from LONGING to BELONGING

Jeannine Higgins

From Longing to Belonging

This is a true story, recalled from notes, records, images and the memory of the author. Every attempt was made to ensure all people, places and events (both past and present) are represented as accurately as possible.

Library of Congress Cataloging-in-Publication data is available

ISBN: 978-1-955077-69-9

10 9 8 7 6 5 4 3 2 1
First printing edition 2021

East 26th Publishing
Houston, TX

This book is dedicated to

Natalia, Tatyana, and Elena for your courageous acts of love.

Thank you for giving the girls life and enabling us to create our family.

from LONGING to BELONGING

PROLOGUE

Hotel Ukraina, Moscow, Russia
November 22, 1998

Michael took us upstairs to our room through the cavernous hallways of the massive, old hotel. In the main room of our two-room suite, there was an empty refrigerator with its door propped open. It was joined by a tired and worn velvet couch, a table and chairs, and a desk. With its high ceilings, huge drafty windows and parquet floor, the room was anything but cozy. The bedroom had two of the smallest "twin" beds we had ever seen. They were very narrow with shiny gold bedspreads and so short that our feet hung over the wooden footboard.

Terry and I nervously sat down on the couch while Michael sat in a chair. He opened his leather valise and asked us for the cashier's check and the ten thousand dollars in cash we carried in our concealed money belts. We handed it over.

We asked him a series of questions, "We just met you an hour ago at the airport and somehow we trust you, but what if you get hit by a bus when you leave here? How will anyone know we gave you the money? Can we have a receipt?"

"Uh. No. That's not how we do business here," he responded without a smile. He stood up and left with our money, saying he'd see us in a few days.

Stunned, Terry and I looked at each other and I thought, O*h my god, what if we were just victims of the world's biggest scam*? As a salve for my rising panic and fear, I joked that we would be profiled on a newsmagazine show like *20/20* or *Dateline* and American TV viewers would think, *How dumb are those two idiots!?*

Chapter ONE

Terry and I were high school sweethearts. He hates that label but how else do you describe two people who have been together since they were freshmen in high school, who were both born and raised in the same South Buffalo neighborhood, grew up together, had the same group of friends and now shared memories of countless formative life experiences?

We dated for twelve years and those years were filled with abundant laughter and joy, vibrancy and potential. We had so much fun in high school; he was at Bishop Timon and I was at Mount Mercy. We drew a competitive spirit out in each other, whether we were playing backgammon, racing on our bikes, or comparing our grades in school. It seemed we turned just about everything into a competition. We were happy for each other's successes and cheered each other on, but we'd jokingly imply we could do just as well ourselves!

We did well in high school and Terry went on to Canisius College while I attended St. Bonaventure. Despite the separate colleges, we managed to keep things together for the most part. Sometimes we'd go our separate ways and date other people, but we'd end up coming back together over spring breaks in Ft. Lauderdale or over the summer in Angola, NY where both of our families had summer cottages.

After college, Terry earned a law degree at UB and I started my career in banking, getting my MBA at Canisius in the evenings. We still hung around with our same childhood friends and enjoyed laughter-filled weekends with them, mostly in local South Buffalo bars and at an apartment I shared with my friend, MaryBeth. Terry excelled in law school, passed the New York State Bar Exam on his first try and embarked on his law career. We both worked long hours and achieved early career successes. We worked downtown and regularly met for lunch. Sometimes, on Fridays, we stopped at happy hour together with friends.

On a hot, humid and breezy day in July 1991, we had a storybook wedding at the Canisius College Chapel, complete with twelve bridal party members, beautiful pink and white flowers and trumpet players from the Buffalo Philharmonic Orchestra. The wedding was followed by a reception with four hundred guests at the newly renovated Statler Golden Ballroom. We attended to many memorable small touches like flaming Baked Alaska for dessert, which was set aflame and paraded around the room by white-gloved servers to the sound system blasting *Feeling Hot, Hot, Hot*. During dinner, instead of the traditional clinking of wine glasses to get the bride and groom to share a kiss, guests were asked to stand and sing a bar of a song that contained the word "love" in its lyrics. A cousin began singing *God Bless America* and the whole crowd leapt to its feet, joined in and bellowed out the entire song, while waving their white cloth napkins. The atmosphere was celebratory and fun! For years, many people remarked that it was such a fun evening. Everyone danced and most guests stayed until the very end. More than a few times that night, a guest would stop us and say, "Finally you two got married!" A few days later, we went on a beautiful honeymoon at a high-end resort in Bermuda, where we enjoyed a relaxing week of sun, sand and sea.

We bought a charming house in South Buffalo five doors down from my parents on Arbour Lane. We also bought a small, fully furnished summer cottage on Lakeside Road near our families' places. I was very familiar with the property because it was my friend Noelle's girlhood cottage and I spent a lot of time there growing up.

Terry and I worked long hours and most days we drove together to work downtown. I am an early riser while Terry is a night owl. I always seemed to be dressed and ready for work before he was. In those days, there was no such thing as casual attire for work and we were both required to wear business suits every day. In the winter, I'd go out in my dress coat and leather dress boots and brush the snow off the car. He'd eventually come out, reach down, grab a snowball and lob it at me, laughing. There'd be a big white snow patch on my wool coat or on the back of my freshly blown-dry hair. Sometimes I'd unsuccessfully try to throw one back at him but sometimes I got annoyed and complained, and then he'd simply say, "I don't like your attitude" and chuckle as he hopped in the driver's seat.

We socialized every weekend and enjoyed our Buffalo Bills season tickets, making a whole day affair out of each game, tailgating in the morning, attending the game and watching the post-game show at various friends' and family members' houses. Those were the Bills' "glory years" and we even went with a dozen friends to the Super Bowl in Atlanta. We traveled every Easter to Florida for vacation with family and every August to Saratoga for the horse races with our friends. We had a big family, and a lot of friends, love, and fun. Life was carefree, things came easy for us, and we felt invincible.

In 1994, we were thirty years old and living a wonderful life when we decided it was finally time to start a family. We had so much love to share. We thought we would be good parents because we were mentally, emotionally and physically well. We had the resources and the capacity to provide a stable, loving and enriching life for a child. At that point, we had nearly two dozen nieces and nephews, which provided us plenty of experience being around young kids.

I looked ahead and wondered what would the two of us be like without a family of our own? Suddenly, our lives seemed to be missing something. When we made the decision to start a family, I began to romanticize being a parent and our "fantasy child" took shape in my imagination. This baby would only possess our collective positive personality and physical traits and none of our undesirable qualities! We were excited, happy and energized. We believed this new stage would be smooth and come just as easy to us as everything else had in the past.

But it didn't happen like we imagined. Just like an upbeat song playing loudly over a speaker that unexpectedly and abruptly stops, so too did our dreams.

We spent the next four years in a dark, sad place—one that tested our relationship and resolve like never before. We went down a challenging path of infertility treatments that were dehumanizing, expensive, embarrassing, painful and time-consuming. We were tossed into a repetitive cycle of anticipation and hope, followed by crushing defeat and despair.

As these monthly cycles melted into four years, our desire for a family turned into desperation and a constant ache. Up until that point, we led charmed lives and faced very little adversity. Up until then, we were able to control most aspects of our lives and, in turn, we controlled our destiny. This loss of control was difficult for us and adjusting to the idea was very challenging. There were moments I was consumed with tears, anger, resentment and sadness.

We left no stone unturned in our quest to have a biological baby. Our daily lives turned into a tornado of appointments, tests, medications, bloodwork and sonograms. These took place at my doctor's office, labs, and at our specialists' offices at Children's and Kenmore Mercy Hospitals. I had several procedures, one surgery and needed daily injections, which Terry gave me. He had to practice on an orange to muster his courage. On the night of the first injection, we were both too scared, so on our way to a party, we stopped at Paula's house in North Buffalo so that she could give me the injection. She was a nurse from Kenmore Mercy Hospital who took pity on us that morning and offered to help when she sensed our uncertainty. I felt no shame and was so thankful for her compassion. The next time, we quickly took care of the injection business in the bathroom while Caitlin, our fifth-grade niece who visited us frequently, played "office" in our spare room. We didn't want to frighten her so we quickly and silently did what needed to be done. We got better at the injections as time went along.

Unwilling to accept the possibility that we couldn't have children, we sought treatment and advice from specialists in Buffalo and Rochester. We then explored emerging technology offered at progressive clinics in California and Virginia. I never kept track of the resources, time and money we spent on our journey. One day, we had a conference call with a clinic in Virginia and the doctor's questions were all about our income and debt. He asked nothing about our health. We realized he was determining our ability to pay for the expensive and novel procedure we were considering. Along the way, we even had a family member offer to act as a surrogate and another who offered her eggs. Such profound gestures, but we refused their generous offers. We continued without openly sharing our pain other than with a select few. We soldiered on in silence, watching our friends build their families. We guarded our privacy. As a result, the stress was taking a toll on my mental health. It was unhealthy to keep it all bottled up. Today, people seem more likely to share news of miscarriages and failed infertility treatments. Back then, people just didn't talk about it. I felt myself slipping into a prolonged state of agitation and depression.

The stress of the infertility treatments was amplified by trying to schedule in the various appointments while working full-time at demanding jobs. I remember being at Children's Hospital for a particularly invasive procedure only to race back to work to begin facilitating an eight a.m. meeting, all the while acting as if I didn't have a care in the world.

We did find a little humor, once in a while. One time, we sat in a clinic waiting room with a man who was very unusual looking. We joked that if I had a baby that looked like that guy, we'd know the clinic messed up something. There were other funny moments, but they are too embarrassing and private to talk about here.

I prayed daily, begging God to help me get pregnant. When our doctor suggested adoption, we promptly dismissed the notion. We knew a couple who had adopted a baby only to have the birth mother change her mind three months after the baby was placed in their arms. No, we didn't want to invite that uncertainty or heartbreak into our lives.

In the midst of all this, we bought our "dream house" in Orchard Park. After a few months, it felt too large for just the two of us. I told Terry that the silence was echoing throughout the high ceilings and if we didn't fill that house with a family soon, I wanted to sell.

One winter day, Terry found a white baby shoe on the slushy sidewalk in downtown Buffalo. It was such an odd place to find a single pristine baby shoe. He brought it home for me and I accepted it as a talisman and cherish it to this day.

The four years of infertility treatments were beginning to take a toll on us. Ever so subtly, I noticed we began to drift apart. Were we working longer hours and socializing separately more often. I was sullen, agitated and depressed. Terry just got quiet.

In the early spring of 1998, I attended a meeting at Baker Victory Services in Lackawanna in my role as the Director of Community Relations at Bell Atlantic. On the walls of the conference room that sunny day, there were several large photos of beautiful Caucasian, Asian and Latino children. I knew Baker Victory was a social services agency, but I didn't know exactly what they did. Captivated, I inquired about the photos and Joe and Beth from Baker Victory responded, "They're newly adopted kids from our international adoption program." What?! How had I never heard of this before? Although Terry and I dismissed the idea of domestic adoption, I immediately and completely became interested in this international program, where the laws governing adoptions were different from the US domestic adoption laws. Those glossy photos were a harbinger of what was in store for us and would change the trajectory of our lives.

While driving home, I had a moment of clarity and realized I had been praying for the wrong thing. I had been praying to get pregnant, when all along, all we wanted was a baby—our baby!

I eagerly dove into research about the international adoption program and became increasingly excited. But there was a glitch. Terry and I were cautious and pragmatic people. We weren't risk takers. We played by societal rules and didn't do anything too bold. We were reluctant and wary of the idea. It was so different—we didn't know anyone who had done it. So much could go wrong and the process was so difficult and overwhelming. It all sounded so scary.

As a result of our uncertainty, we decided to inquire about Baker Victory's domestic adoption program, despite our original reluctance. We were placed on their waiting list for a baby—a disappointing and horribly long eight-year wait. We would be forty-two years old by then. That wasn't a viable solution.

Weeks passed and I began warming up to the idea of adoption. We confided in our lifelong friends, Noelle and Lefty. I grew up with Noelle at the cottage and Terry grew up with Lefty on Edgewood in South Buffalo and they ended up getting married to each other. We were in their wedding party and they were in ours. I told Noelle that Terry needed a little nudge to move ahead with the idea of international adoption. That weekend, Lefty met Terry for a beer and provided encouragement and support for the idea. Terry worried aloud about unknown gene pools, to which Lefty responded, "Who do you think you are, Secretariat?" That quip gave Terry newfound energy and confidence in exploring the idea of international adoption.

A few weeks later in May, there was an ad in our weekly newspaper, announcing Baker Victory's international adoption seminar at a downtown hotel and we decided to attend. People who recently adopted children from Russia, China and Guatemala spoke of their experiences and many brought their newly adopted children with them.

While there, in the crowded room of inquiring prospective parents, a beautiful Russian girl about six or seven years old who had been recently adopted wandered over and climbed onto Terry's lap. This smiling girl embodied hope and gave us a glimpse into our potential future. Terry looked over at me and whispered, "Let's go to Russia and get a baby of our own." Four weeks later, by the grace of God, our perfect little Marissa Jeannine was born on June 4, 1998 nearly five thousand miles away in Murom, Russia.

Chapter TWO

Once we made the decision, we both were immediately and completely invested in the idea of adopting a baby. We shifted gears and began the Russian adoption process. We contacted Baker Victory Services, who would act as our social work agency and they, in turn, put us in contact with the international adoption agency they used. It was called European Adoption Consultants (EAC) and they operated out of Cleveland, Ohio.

It was a new program. The Soviet Union dissolved in 1991 and Westerners began to adopt babies from the newly formed Russian Federation shortly thereafter in 1993. I made a commitment to myself to do something each day that moved us closer to our goal of adopting a baby.

It's difficult to exaggerate the overwhelming amount of paperwork, red tape and bureaucracy we had to wade through. The Department of Justice required background checks, passports, fingerprints and forms. This meant taking time off work and getting an appointment at the Immigration and Naturalization office on Delaware Avenue. Baker Victory met with us during the evening to prepare the required home study, which focused on the safety and suitability of our home. They also assessed our capability as potential parents. For EAC, we needed to dig up or obtain financial statements, medical reports, and background clearances from the Orchard Park Police Department. We also had to provide our tax returns from the past three years.

All this took time and the steps never seemed to go as smoothly as we thought they would. On our lunch hour one day, Terry and I went to Buffalo City Hall together to get the required certified copies of our marriage license and birth certificates. I laughed, reminded of an incident we had in that Office of Vital Statistics seven years prior, getting our birth certificates to go on our honeymoon. An older gentleman waited on us on and appeared at the counter with Terry's birth certificate, which had his name listed as "Baby Boy Higgins." I howled laughing and Terry was annoyed. He asked the man to provide a new one with his full name on it. The man took the birth certificate, painted White-Out over the typewritten "Baby Boy" and wrote "Terrance Patrick" in perfect school-age cursive in the still-wet white goo. Terry's jaw dropped open; his name was spelled incorrectly! When told this, the man picked up a pen and wrote an "e" over the "a" in Terrence so many times that the document nearly had a hole in it.

"Here you go," he said with a shrug.

Terry's face had the stunned expression of the fastidious person he is. I laughed some more.

Sure enough, the certified copy we received for the foreign dossier had the handwritten "Terrence" on it. I thought, "Now how in the world are we going to present THIS to the Russian government as an official document?"

Well, we did and we never heard another word about it. After that, some of us referred to Terry as "Baby Boy" once in a while. It always got a few laughs. Grandma Dot, Terry's mother, provided some background: Terry was born a few weeks after John F. Kennedy was assassinated and Papa Jim, his father, floated the idea of naming the baby after JFK. Dot wasn't so keen on this idea and, needless to say, Terry left the hospital without being named and that explains why the birth certificate was on file as "Baby Boy" for twenty-seven years.

We marched on, assembling our paperwork. We needed to provide proof of our employment, the deed to our home, proof of medical insurance, three lengthy letters of reference from friends and the names and addresses of all our combined ten siblings. EAC also required a list of every single address we ever lived at for our entire lives, including my college flop house at St. Bonaventure. When I called a few of them, none of my roommates could remember the exact address, but we enjoyed reminiscing about the fun we had while living there. I ended up fudging the house number on that one.

One night, Terry told me a funny story about getting his medical clearance earlier that day. He went to his childhood pediatrician, who was smoking a cigarette as he "examined" Terry and completed the required medical form. The doctor whispered, "Terry can you hear me?" and "How about now?" in an even lower whisper. Yes, Terry could hear him and so the hearing test box on the form was summarily checked off.

Once we got the mountain of paperwork together, we had to make two copies of each page and send them along with the various fees and certifications as our "foreign dossier" to EAC (European Adoption Consultants) in Ohio. Then it all had to be forwarded to the Russian Ministry of Education who handled adoptions "on the ground" in Russia.

A foreign dossier? We had never heard of that before. According to The Hague Convention, any official document provided to a foreign government must be notarized. Ok, that was easy. Every attorney in Terry's office was a notary. We'd ask one of them to do it. After that, we had to bring each document to the Erie County Clerk's office for certification of the notary, which cost three dollars per page. That meant a lengthy trip to County Hall during business hours with a stack of papers. Then, everything was sent to the New York State Department of State in Albany for an "apostille" to be attached to each document, which was ten dollars per page, payable with a certified check from the bank. Whew. The State of New York had to certify that the County of Erie was legitimate and the County of Erie had to certify that the Notary was valid. This "checking the checkers" seemed crazy to us, but we did it. The county stamped the form and stapled a small blue sheet to each of our original pages. New York State stamped the county's form and stapled a white paper to that. And we needed two copies of everything. All this additional paper and staples made our foreign dossier about ten inches thick.

Once it was completed, we forwarded the dossier to EAC in Ohio, using FedEx because it was a traceable system. Because we spent so much time, money and effort preparing the paperwork, we were afraid of it getting lost and even discussed driving the stack of papers down to EAC in Cleveland ourselves. But, we settled on FedEx after all. If we accepted a referral for a baby, the U.S. Embassy in Russia and the Russian Consulate in the United States would then both require additional paperwork to be completed. Most families adopted within two to nine months after completion of their dossier.

The various fees due along the way all had vague names like registration fee, preliminary application fee, dossier fee, international program processing fee and so on. The amounts seemed large and arbitrary and closed in on ten thousand dollars but we were in no position to comparison-shop or check prices. Here we were—two intelligent, cautious people paying all those fees, all while operating on faith and hope alone. We always thought infertility treatments were expensive, time consuming and complicated! Turns out, that was just a warm up!

During May and June of 1998, we completed the paperwork, kept focused on each step, and tried not to get overwhelmed. The paperwork process was slow and cumbersome compared to today's standards because 1998 was before the digital age—pre-Google, pre-laptops and pre-smartphones. Like most people, we had dial-up internet access and used a free CD from AOL as our web browser. Back then, once you did get online, there wasn't much to see. There were no online forms to complete, no PDFs to fill, no text messages to send, no attachments to email or documents to scan. Everything arrived in the mail as blank paper forms, which we completed with a pen, whiting out any mistakes we made. I made copies at work or the library and once it was all done, sent it to the agency via FedEx. Our questions had to be answered with a phone call to the agency and the "phone tag" game always ensued, making me nervous about missing a call. You get the picture: the paperwork process took a LOT longer than it would today.

We were afraid of something going wrong, so we chose not to tell many people until the paperwork was completed and we were approved as "adoption ready" by the Russian and U.S. governments and EAC.

We were approved in July and a picture of Terry and I was placed on EAC's "Magic Wall," which is where you stayed while you waited for a referral for a baby. The Russians would send EAC a photo and a little medical information about a baby and the agency would go to the "Magic Wall" and see if a match could be made. The match was based partly on prospective parents' requests. For example: We requested an infant, the gender didn't matter, and we'd consider multiples. Some people wanted older children to fit in with their already-established families and their ages. Some people specifically requested children with special needs and others were only looking for multiples.

One warm, mid-July evening on the back porch of the Higgins family cottage, we decided to tell our extended family of our plans to adopt. Hugs, kisses, a few tears and lots of congratulations followed. We clarified: we were going to Russia to adopt. Russia? People had so many questions and what answers we DID have were vague and uncertain.

"Are you sure?" they asked, to which all we could say was a semi-convincing, "Yes, we are sure."

The conversations over the coming weeks all had the same themes around our safety, the cost, the process, the risk and the uncertainty.

If our family and friends thought we were foolish, no one said it out loud to us. In retrospect, it was obvious that their tolerance for uncertainty was nowhere near the shockingly high level of ours. So, we forged ahead with hope in our hearts and we settled in to wait. And wait.

Meanwhile, we talked with Baker Victory Services, EAC and families who had already traveled to Russia and we read what little we could find about Russian orphanages. We discovered stories about babies and children living in deplorable conditions, which filled us with sadness and despair. A few years prior, there had been a widely viewed documentary on the squalid conditions in Romanian orphanages. We struggled to keep our imaginations from drawing parallels. All the information we accumulated fueled our angst and sense of urgency, making the long wait for a referral torturous. We prayed to God, asking Him to protect our yet-to-be-selected baby and I wrote undelivered letters to the baby, telling him or her to hold on for just a little while longer. Mommy and Daddy were coming soon.

I started that cool, sunny September day at a United Way meeting followed by a radio interview on WBEN. That afternoon, I was in my office on the eleventh floor of 65 Franklin Street overlooking Lake Erie when my phone rang.

"Bell Atlantic, Jeannine Higgins."

"Jeannine, it's Claire from EAC."

I drew a blank for a second. This was a voice and name I had never heard before. OH MY GOD! This is the call we've been waiting for! I sat down and grabbed a pen and paper.

"We have a baby for you and she's young," said Claire. "We never get them this young. She was born on June fourth."

Wait. Did Claire say, "She?!" It was a girl!

Claire continued, "Her name is Olga Rusheva. She's three months old and she was bottle fed her whole life. Her mother gave up her rights at birth."

Claire pronounced the baby's name as *Ole-Ga* and that's how we said it until we received a VCR tape of the baby two days later and heard a Russian lady pronounce the much softer, prettier *Ole-ya*. The baby was in an orphanage called Murom Infant Home in the Vladimir Region, a few hours drive outside of Moscow. I was relieved. That meant no Russian airline flights. Russia is the largest country in the world and crosses eleven time zones. It is divided into regions, much like the United States is divided into states. We had heard horror stories about long airline flights in Russia to orphanages in Siberia, and we were hoping to avoid that.

I immediately called Terry at work, but he was busy so he placed me on hold. I was pacing in my office.

"We got a call from EAC. They have a baby for us," I blurted when he picked up and then I went through the details. He quietly listened.

"I'm nervous," he responded when I asked him about his lack of excitement.

After talking a few minutes Terry announced, "Well, her name is going to be Marissa Jeannine. She's my little Marissa."

A few days later, we received a VCR tape, a brief medical report and a small picture that didn't show her face very well. We met Terry's parents for dinner at a restaurant on the lake. We told them about the baby and showed them the photo. They were thrilled for us. Finally, this adoption idea had gone from being abstract to something real.

At home that night we watched the one-minute video of Marissa Jeannine in her orphanage for the first of a hundred times. We watched it after work quite often and, if we went out for dinner and drinks, we'd watch it when we came home. Getting ready for work in the morning now included at least one viewing of the video. The video was too fleeting and each time we watched it, we were left wanting more. It was grainy footage and we couldn't determine her eye color but it showed a strong, curious and beautiful baby. We both fell in love with that baby, watching the video over and over and over again.

Marissa's medical report listed "perinatal post-hypoxic encephalopathy; myotonic syndrome, and moderate diffuse muscular hypotonia." Loosely translated, this meant she had an acute brain injury due to lack of oxygen at birth, along with a long-term genetic disorder that causes muscle loss and weakness. She also had decreased muscle tone.

We read and reread the baby's "medical" report. We were cautioned about these reports by EAC and Baker Victory. Sometimes the reports contained diagnoses that the Western medical community didn't use. The agency told us that in their opinion, the Russian orphanage medical directors used ominous-sounding diagnoses that were fabricated because the Russian government didn't want healthy babies being adopted by foreigners and leaving the country. These medical directors knew that getting these children out of the orphanages and into families was paramount, so they prepared falsified medical reports to enable that to happen. Sometimes, the reports had misinformation due to poor language translation.

Completely out of character for us, we decided to ignore the medical report. This was based on EAC's guidance and, as a result, we relied solely on what we observed in Marissa's video. She looked wonderful and, in fact, that scary medical report turned out to be not only incorrect, but ironic. The coming months and years would reveal that she didn't lack muscle strength or tone but, to the contrary, she had exceptional athleticism. She walked at ten months, rode a two-wheeled bike at three years old, and was on a competitive ice hockey team at age six, culminating in playing on an NCAA Division I women's ice hockey team.

A few days after receiving the referral, we called EAC and accepted. Olga (Marissa) was our baby. Now we had to wait for the Russian government's approval and a travel date, which could take up to six months.

In the meantime, Baker Victory required us to take parenting classes with other couples traveling to Russia to adopt. A couple from Hamburg was getting two babies. Another couple from Hamburg was getting an infant girl and already had two biological boys. A South Buffalo couple was getting an older child to be playmates with their nine-year-old domestically adopted daughter. And an Eden couple was getting a boy—their first child. We formed an informal support group and became friendly. Several months later, when we were all back home with our kids, Terry and I had everyone over for a party at our house to share our experiences and celebrate together.

The parenting classes focused on bathing, changing and feeding babies. It was geared to teenage girls who were preparing to be babysitters! We laughed at the ridiculousness of it all, especially the people who were already parents.

While the infant and children CPR portion was helpful, the classes did absolutely nothing to prepare us for the challenges that lay ahead. They never discussed Fetal Alcohol Syndrome, Reactive Attachment Disorder, Post Traumatic Stress Disorder, abandonment issues, or health issues like rickets and parasitic infections. The parenting class didn't give any advice about transitioning from the orphanage to home and they didn't talk about various institutional behaviors that some parents in our group would come to see. We learned later that most kids adopted from Russia, particularly older ones, all suffered from some of these conditions, syndromes or issues.[1] Parenting them wouldn't necessarily be easy. Remember the Russian girl who climbed on Terry's lap at the informational seminar that past May? We discovered that her behavior was symptomatic of something called "institutional autism" where the child displays indiscriminate friendliness and affection. She may have gone home with anyone in the seminar room that day. Lastly, the parenting classes made no mention of the possible effects on our own emotional and psychological well-being from visiting a Russian orphanage and parenting a child who experienced neglect and trauma.

During the last twenty years, we've had periodic conversations with the parents in that class and we realized that some of us had smoother rides parenting our kids then others.

The September days following Marissa's referral dragged by and our thoughts became obsessive. Were they holding her? Were they feeding her? What was she doing? Was she waking up at night? What if she got sick? Our anxiety was building. What if her birth mother changed her mind or what if a Russian couple adopted her in the meantime?

Those fears, we discovered, were well-founded. After the Soviet Union dissolved in 1991, Russian laws, including adoption laws, were set by their newly formed parliament or, Duma. It seemed to us that the Duma was apt to change the laws quickly, often, and arbitrarily. We would be at the mercy of the Duma and its seemingly random ways many times over the next five years.

Our agency explained that some Duma members were concerned about the "brain drain" from Russia. They wanted those orphaned children to stay in Russia to continue to grow their country's population, prosperity and power. Perhaps they wanted the boys for the military—an idea whispered to us by the Russians we met. A large majority of the children were called "social orphans," meaning they had at least one living parent.

One Russian law stated that an orphaned child had to be placed in the Russian national database for six months before being released for adoption by an international family. That six month time period gave Russian families ample opportunity to adopt the child, which was something they rarely did. We were told that the Russian people valued family and loved children, but there was a deep-seated and widespread stigma and aversion to adopting children. As a culture, they had this idea (which seemed bizarre to us) that something must be mentally and emotionally "wrong" for a woman to give up her child for adoption, and the orphaned child inherited this condition so, therefore, the child was also mentally ill and viewed as damaged goods. Also, in 1998, thirty percent of the nation was living at or below the poverty level.[2] People simply could not afford to adopt. Still, some members of the Russian government did not want healthy babies leaving the country in droves. According to the Russian adoption coordinators we spoke with, poverty was a main reason for women giving up their babies. In post-Soviet Russia in 1998, there were little to no social safety nets such as welfare, non-profit organizations, social services, foster care systems and church groups helping the community. Under the old Soviet regime, the people had been taken care of by the government and now, eighty years later, they were left on their own.[3] Inflation was rampant and the cost of living soared. A few oligarchs got very wealthy but many Russians fell into deep poverty. Interestingly, at that time, birth control was NOT available but abortions were common, free and widely accessible.[4] So an impoverished pregnant woman who was morally opposed to abortion was left with few options.

At the time, all reports indicated there were over six hundred thousand children and babies living in Russian orphanages. Thousands lived on the streets in large cities like Moscow and they were referred to as "street urchins," some of whom ended up here in Western New York. Just like we have a public library in most towns, Russia had an orphanage in most towns and those orphanages were overcrowded and underfunded.[5]

Marissa was only three months old when she was referred to us and we had to wait for her to get off the national database when she turned six months old. I'd often wake up in the middle of the night with fear and anxiety about her.

While waiting for Marissa during the fall of 1998, Sarah McLachlan had a popular song, "In the Arms of an Angel" on the radio. It brought me to tears every time I heard it because it seemed to speak directly to Marissa with its haunting sound and lyrics, "...you spend all your time waiting for that second chance…for a break that'll make it okay. In the arms of an angel fly away from here."

On September 28, eighteen days after we received Marissa's referral, Claire from EAC called me at eleven o'clock in the morning and left a voicemail. At noon, I returned the call and sheer panic washed over me as I dialed. My mind went to the absolute worst case scenario.

"Hi Claire. Do you have good news or bad news for me? Tell me immediately!" I blurted when we connected on the phone.

There was nothing to worry about. EAC had another baby for us to consider adopting along with Marissa. It was a baby boy, born prematurely on May 4, 1998. He was exactly one month older than Marissa. I told Claire to send us his medical report and video and we would make our decision. So many thoughts ran through my mind. Would we raise them as twins because they were so close in age? Would they like that? Would socialization at home be good for them? Could we handle two babies at once? I called Terry at work.

"Are you sitting down? Do you have a minute?" I asked.

"No and yes," he answered.

"EAC has another baby for us. It's a boy, one month older than Marissa."

He sounded different than when I called him about Marissa. The nervousness and uncertainty I heard from him before were replaced with laughter and excitement.

He said, "Have them send the video and we will decide if it's right for Marissa."

When we accepted Marissa's referral, it was scary, exhilarating and exciting. Rejecting the referral for the baby boy was just sad. We made the decision not to adopt him based on our gut feeling. It just didn't seem right. Being premature, he appeared to have more medical issues than we felt capable of handling. We knew our limitations and wanted Marissa to have one hundred percent of us while she adjusted to family life. We didn't want to shortchange her. She had lived in an orphanage alone for this long and we didn't want to divide our parental attention. I found it amazing that after just two short weeks, we felt so connected and protective of our new daughter just from looking at a tiny picture and a one-minute video. The love we felt for her filled our hearts and minds. Still, rejecting that little boy's referral was horribly difficult. Mentally, I beat myself up about it.

Were we petty? Would someone else adopt him? EAC assured us that plenty of U.S. families were waiting to become his potential parents. I prayed that God would stand with us and help me realize that rejecting his referral didn't make us bad people.

I tried to refocus and recapture the excitement and love we felt about going to get Marissa. As some retail therapy, I ordered her a little snowsuit from LL Bean. Over the years, when I looked back at the pictures, I often wondered why I didn't order her a pink one. When she left the orphanage, I dressed her in a green and blue snowsuit. I'm no expert in psychology but I wondered if that little boy influenced my snowsuit buying decision and the colors I chose.

We spent October getting ready. We prepared a beautiful, soft and inviting nursery which was decorated in pink and white. Every morning before work, Terry walked into the empty nursery and looked out the window. I never disturbed him, but I knew he was imagining a morning when he'd walk in there, lift Marissa out of her crib and show her the deer in the woods behind our house.

In the beginning of November, we were still waiting to receive a travel date. I was afraid to travel to Russia. We spent our childhoods, participating in air-raid drills in elementary schools, where a loud siren would sound and we were instructed to crouch under our desks. These were practice drills in case the Russians ever bombed us. I knew the Cold War had ended, but old ways of thinking are difficult to shake. I was also scared to go to Russia because it was so far away. There was no way to stay connected to people at home. This was before any internet connection, iPhone text messages, or social media platforms. We'd be out of touch with our families while we were there and our agency told us it was not a safe place to travel. Beyond that, we also had anxiety about the orphanage and the baby. We wondered if we would frighten the baby with our foreign voices, our new faces and our unfamiliar smells. The waiting was agonizing. Marissa was teaching us about patience, bravery and unconditional love.

Chapter THREE

Two weeks later, we were notified that Marissa would be removed from the database on November 17 and we would travel to Moscow that coming Saturday, November 21 to get her. Now, there were several more documents to complete for the U.S. and Russian embassies. To apply for our visas we had to move quickly and send:

- our ORIGINAL passports
- visa application forms
- two passport pictures for each of us
- a special form for Terry (why? I don't know)
- money orders payable to the Russian embassy
- a FedEx envelope
- a prepaid airbill back to us marked for Saturday delivery
- a twenty-dollar personal check payable to someone named Olga in Potomac, MD, for her courier fee

Yes, we had five days to apply and receive back our Russian travel visas. All this had to be done while working full-time, packing and getting ready. I planned to take a one-year leave of absence from my job, so I had a lot of loose ends to tie up at work. The pressure was incredible and my stress and anxiety were skyrocketing.

The phones at work and home were ringing off the hook with friends, acquaintances and family, all wishing us well. They asked if they could help. They'd inquire about the packing but, really, they wanted to share in the excitement of it all. Adopting a baby from Russia was such a novel idea and people were very curious and had all kinds of questions. Our friends bought us a video camera so we could capture Marissa's first days with us. Marissa was coming home to two parents, four grandparents, twenty three cousins, nineteen aunts and uncles and countless friends.

We'd never experienced anything like it before. We received over one hundred gifts from family, friends, colleagues and acquaintances. Cards and notes were arriving daily in the mail. The whole community was excited about this baby! People threw me three baby showers—one was a total surprise. People we barely knew were sending us cards, tokens and well wishes. Gifts, clothes, toys, books, Mass cards, crosses and rosaries came from friends, family, coworkers, professional colleagues, acquaintances and "friends of friends" who heard our story. My mother always stressed the importance of timely, handwritten thank you cards, but in the frenzied weeks leading up to our trip, I knew I'd have to wait until we returned to take care of that task.

This was before emails, blogging or Facebook, but the word spread like wildfire. The generosity, interest and excitement was overwhelming. People in Western New York and South Buffalo were touched by Marissa's story. She was like a baby celebrity before she ever arrived in Buffalo!

Ten days before we left, I attended a Neil Diamond concert downtown with my mother and sisters. When he sang his popular anthem, *America*, we got on our feet, sang along and all felt chills and I shed some happy tears. His lyrics were so fitting. "Far. We've been traveling far. On a boat and on a plane, they're coming to America. Never looking back again, they're coming to America." It was a thrilling and exhilarating moment for me.

We felt such pride in America, our flag and in our freedom and everyone in our circle of family and friends was happy that Marissa would be coming to America for the opportunity of a better life.

By the second week of November, Marissa's supplies were laid out all over our living room floor—bottles, sleepers, blankets, rattles, formula, diapers, wipes, etc. I even packed an electric tea kettle to boil water to make her bottles in Russia. We also had our own things to pack. I borrowed a striped sweater from my friend Maureen because I figured it would match with everything and I planned to wear it daily. It was the only sweater I packed. It was freezing cold in Russia and we needed warm clothes. Terry packed a black fur hat that our sister-in-law, Lina, gave him from her days as a U.S. Border Patrol agent. It looked like a real Russian *shapka*, or so we thought.

In addition to the many fees we already paid, we had to go to the bank and get ten thousand dollars in new U.S. currency that was sequentially numbered. I remember filling out a large currency transaction report (CTR) at the bank, which our government requires any time someone wants a sum of cash exceeding ten thousand dollars, the purpose of which was to uncover any money laundering schemes. Terry remembers the dollar amount being eighteen thousand but my notes indicate ten thousand dollars.

We were told by our agency to bring this cash to Russia, split between us in concealed money belts. Terry carried his portion of the cash in a pouch around his neck under his clothes and I wore mine in a belt hidden around my waist. We were also told not to declare this at customs in the Russian airport when we arrived. This money was in addition to an official bank cashier's check we had to bring. It was for six thousand dollars, payable to someone whose name escapes me now. The directive about the new U.S. currency concealed on our bodies was so out of character for us. We were rule followers our whole lives and never did anything considered the least bit "shady." The thought of carrying this large amount of cash was extremely unsettling, making us feel more vulnerable than the process itself already did.

The week we were leaving, EAC called me and gave us a list of "gifts" we had to bring to Russia. This caused quite a bit of discussion among family and friends. "Is this bribery?" we were repeatedly asked.

It was explained to us that no, it was not technically bribery. Gift giving was the accepted way of doing business in Russia at that time. Under the Communist regime, the average citizen had very little access to the kinds of consumer goods and amenities we took for granted. It was also difficult to get things done there, so gifts from the Western world kept the adoption process moving. We had to bring an extra-large ladies bathrobe, two bottles of Dewar's Scotch and a silver Cross pen and pencil set, which was an expensive luxury item most often seen on the desks of American corporate executives. They wanted soap but didn't identify a brand, just "the good smelling kind." We also had to bring a suitcase packed full with dozens of pairs of shoes and clothes for the orphanage, two cartons of U.S.-

made Marlboro Lights and a Little Tykes Cozy Coupe car. We would NOT be traveling light! A little lighter than some people, though. One poor couple had to bring a set of snow tires.

We borrowed an old suitcase from my mother's friend Flossie's attic. She told us to leave the suitcase over in Russia. We piled the orphanage gifts into the old suitcase and opened the large Little Tykes box and stuffed the other gifts inside.

We Duct-taped the box up and packed Marissa's suitcase. We had to bring business attire for our court appearance, which meant suits for Terry and me in a garment bag and dress shoes for the both of us. We also brought along some snacks for us to eat while there. We got that ready, packed our suitcases and we were ready to roll. It was crazy the amount of stuff we had to lug over there.

Our travel arrangements were made by Norm, a travel agent in Ohio that EAC used regularly. We'd fly to JFK in New York Saturday morning and then take the nine-and-a-half hour flight to Moscow that night. Our airfare was two thousand dollars per person.

Chapter FOUR

Saturday arrived and our flight to New York was at eight o'clock in the morning. My mother, sister Peggy and a few of her kids came inside the Buffalo airport and because it was pre-9/11, there was no security screening. They walked us to our gate, which was a door that led outside to a small propeller plane. They hugged us, said "stay safe" and we left. There was nothing more we could say. We all had lumps in our throats. I remember being almost dizzy with emotion, mostly fear and anxiety, as I went outside to the awaiting plane.

We arrived at JFK airport in New York at ten o'clock that morning. After retrieving our ridiculous mountain of luggage, we boarded a shuttle bus to the international terminal. That was a struggle! Once there, we sat and waited all day in the empty terminal until we could check in for the international flight at four o'clock that afternoon. Sitting amid piles of luggage, we read the *New York Times* cover-to-cover, and took turns going for food and using the restroom. We were road weary before we even got on the Delta flight to Moscow.

We departed for Moscow on schedule, had dinner on board and I enjoyed a glass of wine. Most people were traveling on business or going to adopt a child. We didn't know it at the time, but that was the first of ten transatlantic flights between the U.S. and Russia that we would take over the next five years. On each of our flights to Moscow, there was a group of loud and boisterous Russian businessmen who stood in the aisles and in the back of the plane and drank vodka the whole way. They never rested and always seemed to be having a great time. Our return flights were nicknamed "baby flights" because of the number of adopted babies on board.

We flew to the Sheremetyevo Airport, which is one of TEN Moscow airports that serve the population of twenty million. Three of them are international and Sheremetyevo is located north of the city center of Moscow.

We landed at ten-thirty, Moscow time Sunday morning and it was sunny and cold, one degree Fahrenheit. It looked beautiful with a coat of freshly fallen snow covering the ground. I imagined the movie set for *Dr. Zhivago*, one of my parents' favorite movies. While waiting to get off the plane, we were excited and we kept saying, "I can't believe we are here," to each other. But reality was setting in. We were in fact, "here."

The airport was quiet, dimly lit and hazy with cigarette smoke. It was such a gloomy, outdated and menacing atmosphere. There were guards, armed with machine guns, walking around in dark green military uniforms, all speaking Russian. We heard a lady's voice over the loudspeaker, making austere sounding announcements we couldn't understand. Over the next five years, we'd often hear loud speakers in Russian train stations, airports and metro stations; the voices were always women. Back then, there was absolutely nothing written in English anywhere. It was all Russian. If we wanted to translate anything, we had to reference a small booklet EAC gave us that listed common phrases.

I was so nervous, afraid and intimidated going through customs with the concealed money belts. My heart was racing, my breathing shallow and my stomach in knots. As we approached, I felt like Dorothy meeting the *Wizard of Oz*. But thankfully, we didn't have any problems and no one questioned us. When I think back on that moment, the amount of unfounded trust we had in the process shocks me. While getting our luggage, we noticed a cat sitting on the baggage carousel. Then we proceeded out toward the main terminal. Before leaving home, EAC told us that a Russian driver who worked with EAC would meet us. If no one was there, we were instructed to wait. They said it might take hours for them to arrive. If the person didn't show up, we were to get a taxicab and go to the hotel. My anxiety was skyhigh and would remain so until our return flight back home.

Much to our relief, we immediately saw a slight man with black hair wearing a leather jacket. He had a sly smile and he held a sign that read "EAC." That was for us! It was Sergei, our driver for the week. He spoke no English. He was accompanied by a blond, youthful-looking guy dressed in an LL Bean barn jacket. He was carrying a leather valise. That was Michael, our Moscow coordinator, whose English was excellent. They were both so friendly and welcoming, making us feel at ease as we settled into Sergei's dark Lada, a small square junky-looking Russian-made car. It looked and had the exhaust smell of a car from the 1970s. Terry was familiar with the make of the vehicle, although I never heard of them before. The airport parking lot was full of them.

"They're shit boxes," Terry whispered to me.

On the one-hour drive to the center of Moscow, Michael kept turning his shoulders around to talk to us in the back seat and he explained the plans for the week. We would stay in Moscow at the Hotel Ukraina until Tuesday. Then we would drive out to the Vladimir Region to get Marissa.

During the drive to the hotel, Terry and I eagerly looked out the window at the strange city which looked so outdated to us. Old trolley-busses, trams, and cars filled the streets. We passed a sea of dreary looking and nondescript Soviet-style apartment buildings. Pedestrians wore drab brown or grey coats with fur hats. The city appeared almost colorless to us, a mix of grays and browns. Even the roads were brown. It snowed before we arrived and the streets were not plowed down to the pavement, but rather they had been sanded, creating a thick layer of "brown-sugar" like slush on the road, obscuring all the lines and lanes. We couldn't decipher organized traffic patterns on the clogged and chaotic eleven-lane road.

The Hotel Ukraina was a massive Soviet-style structure right in the center of the city looming over the Moscow River. It had one thousand hotel rooms. We could tell that at one time, it had been a "grand hotel" but had fallen into disrepair. There were young military guards standing around in the lobby, again armed with machine guns. An old Russian "babushka" grandmother-type was outside in the frigid air, bent over, removing the snow from the front steps and walkway. I remember her sweeping the snow with a broom while Terry remembers her having an old metal shovel. (It's so interesting how Terry and I remember certain details differently.) She was dressed in layers of dark clothing and she didn't look nearly warm enough, young enough, or fit enough to be doing what she was doing.

Michael spoke for us at the front desk and told us we had to give the hotel employee our passports, which the hotel would hold during our stay. We were never told this before and we didn't like the idea at all, but we gave them the passports anyway. While waiting, we glanced around the high ceilinged lobby and realized the hotel had not been updated in decades.

Michael took us upstairs to our room along cavernous hallways that smelled strange. Our two-room suite had a full-sized empty refrigerator with its door propped open in the main room where it was joined by a couch, a table and a desk. The bedroom had two of the smallest "twin" beds we had ever seen. They were very narrow, had gold, shiny bedspreads and were so short that our feet hung over the end.

We sat down on the couch and Michael sat in a chair. He opened his valise and asked us for the cashier's check and all the cash in our money belts. We handed them over.

We asked a series of questions, "We just met you and somehow we trust you, but what if you get hit by a bus on your way out? How will anyone know we gave you the money? Can we have a receipt?"

"Uh. No. That's not how we do business here," he responded.

He left with our money, saying he'd see us in a few days.

Terry and I looked at each other and I thought "Oh my god, what if we were just victims of the world's biggest scam?" We joked that we would show up on a news magazine show like *20/20* or *Dateline* and American TV viewers would think "How dumb are those two idiots?"

We slept most of the day, evening and night. The phone in our room rang about five different times. Each time Terry answered, a Russian girl asked in broken English if he wanted any "company." She was obviously a prostitute who was given our room number by someone working at the hotel. No, he didn't want any company, he told her, getting increasingly adamant and annoyed each time she called. My anxiety was escalating.

On Monday morning, we went down to the brightly-lit and once-beautiful main salon for the included breakfast. I couldn't eat but Terry could. They had a salad bar, fish, sliced meat, boiled eggs and warm milk. I settled for bitter strong coffee and later, the oatmeal I brought from home, made with my electric tea kettle.

I remember showering that morning in the outdated bathroom. We were cautioned by EAC to keep our mouths and eyes closed when showering because their water was contaminated with bacteria and parasites that would surely make us sick. To add to my "already off the charts" anxiety, I was now afraid of getting a parasite, with good reason. More on that concern later. We were also warned that in the hotels, the water was usually turned off for a few hours during the day, so showering in the morning was the best bet.

The day was sunny and cold. We were told we would spend the day on a guided tour of Moscow with EAC's Russian secretary, Oksana. I was consumed with angst about getting Marissa and now we had to spend a day acting as tourists? I remember wishing we would have traveled to Russia a day later and skipped this nonsense. I don't know for sure, but it seemed like EAC received a directive from someone, perhaps the Russian government that they showcase "Mother Russia," a common term of endearment amongst Russian citizens. I'm just guessing at that. But, in the end, I changed my thinking. I was very pleased to get to know Moscow and I look back on that experience with great fondness.

Oksana was a twenty-three-year-old lovely person who was very knowledgeable about Moscow and the history of Russia. Her English was excellent. She enjoyed talking about the rich cultural contributions of their society: the famous Bolshoi Ballet, writers like Dostoevsky and Tolstoy, and composers like Tchaikovsky. Her knowledge of Russian history was impressive. She wore a stunning full length black fur coat with a matching hat. On the streets that day, I noticed that all the women dressed like that. Oksana looked stylish, clean and fresh that day, her hair done and her makeup impeccable. I learned later that the Russians with whom we interacted only bathed once a week, often at public bathhouses. When we saw her four days later, she was still wearing the same sweater and her makeup and hair didn't look quite the same as it had on Monday.

We visited Red Square, the Kremlin and the iconic St. Basil's Cathedral. It was breathtaking against the bright blue sky. We went to Lenin's Tomb and waited in line to get in. It was dark in there and we paraded with the crowd down the slanted hallway. An armed guard scolded Terry in Russian and gestured with his gun for Terry to remove his hat to show respect for Mr. Lenin. We didn't realize it, but the Russians treated this experience like a wake. Lenin was in a glass case with a light shining on him. We couldn't stop long to get a real good look at him, but from what we did see, we both agreed he was a very slight person and looked like wax.

We went on to the famous GUM department store and bought a bottle of top shelf vodka for Terry's friend, Danny. We rode the underground metro system with its renowned beautiful mosaic walls and marble entryways. Last, we visited the Kremlin's Armory Museum, which houses many of Russia's national treasures, including armor, spectacular jewels, bejeweled Faberge eggs, thrones and crowns from the Tsars. We saw the Romanov family's gilded carriage, which was stunning.

That day we learned that Moscow is pronounced a few different ways. Americans pronounce Moscow with the accent on the second syllable, *MosCOW,* like the bovine animal. The Europeans, however, pronounce it, *MUScoe,* with the accent on the first syllable and the c-o-w sounding like the word "coworker." *MUScoe.* The Russians use *Mockba* and pronounce it, *Mask-VA,* with the emphasis on the second syllable. Terry started calling it, *Mock-Ba,* his own unique pronunciation!

During our tour, Oksana explained that decades earlier, Joseph Stalin had the eleven-lane roads constructed in Moscow to enable planes to land on them, if needed, during World War II. After the war, he ordered seven identical skyscrapers called the "Seven Sisters" to be built and the Hotel Ukraina was one of them. They were built to glorify the Soviet State and were supposed to rival the skyscrapers in the United States. Stalin was worried that if people visited Moscow, they'd only see low buildings and would not be impressed, so he ordered these seven identical skyscrapers built. They dominate the Moscow skyline to this day. Moscow University is another one of these "Seven Sisters." My opinion is that image is critically important to the Russian government—then and now.

After buying a few souvenirs, we concluded our time with Oksana. Terry and I both thought it was an interesting and memorable day. We thoroughly enjoyed ourselves, felt safe and we were happy to see the beautiful city, especially in the company of our warm and friendly tour guide, Oksana.

I think it's a good idea to stop here and explain what it was like in the Russian Federation at that time, 1998. The country would change every time we visited over the next five years, the influence of Western culture becoming more pronounced with each visit. By 2003, we were eating cheeseburgers in an American Radisson hotel, emailing people at home with updates, and watching first-run Hollywood movies in the hotel theater. But in 1998, for us, it was like going to another planet, the culture shock hitting us hard. Maybe this was because we were on a mission of adopting a baby and not carefree tourists.

The Soviet Union and its state socialist economy had collapsed seven years earlier in 1991 and the Russian Federation with its capitalist market economy was emerging under the stewardship of the Russian Federation's first president, Boris Yeltsin. The people were stuck between the old system and the new one and in 1998, we were fortunate to bear witness to this unique time in the country's history.

Russia's transformation was difficult and in the 1990s, there were two Chechen wars and a severe financial crisis. State-owned assets such as oil and gas fields were privatized and there were newfound cultural and religious freedoms for the people.

An oligarchical system developed, so while a select few got extraordinarily wealthy, life for the average Russian was very challenging. Thirty percent of the population lived at or below the poverty level. The ruble collapsed and lost seventy percent of its value against the U.S. dollar.[6] We were warned that being stopped by the police was extremely dangerous. (As a side note, being stopped by the police was viewed as very problematic by our agency, so before leaving the U.S., they provided us a "cheat sheet" on what to say and how to respond, should we be stopped.) According to the WHO (World Health Organization), more people died of tuberculosis in 1998 than in any other time in history and they pointed to the Russian Federation as a problem spot. Food was scarce and so were jobs. Some people appeared to be living on the edge of desperation, causing Terry and me to wonder if they had a lingering nostalgia for the old days when their daily lives were more stable and predictable under the old totalitarian Soviet regime.

I found it remarkable that even in the difficult time of 1998, Oksana could be so resilient and possess such personal fortitude. She, and others we would meet had such optimism and showed us warmth and friendliness every day. These were people who accepted the harsh realities of their lives because they deeply loved their country and their culture and they were genuinely pleased to share it with us.

After our delightful day with Oksana was over, we arrived back at the hotel lobby and coincidentally bumped into the Hamburg couple from our parenting class back home! I knew they were traveling but we had no idea we'd see them in Moscow. They had just gotten back from the Russian city of Chita, which was four thousand miles from Moscow on the Mongolian border, where they adopted their two babies. The kids were both sick with colds, but all of them were so happy to be together. It was great to see familiar faces and the chance meeting buoyed all of our spirits and it had a calming effect on me, if only for a little while.

That evening, we had no plans and Terry slept peacefully. I was awake, trying to read a book but mostly spent the time thinking and worrying about our trip to the Vladimir Region in the morning. We were finally going to meet Marissa.

Chapter FIVE

In the hotel lobby the next morning at 6:45 am, we met up with Barb and Loren, a couple from Michigan with whom we would be traveling to the Vladimir Region. They were adopting a baby boy from Marissa's orphanage, which was called the Murom Infant Home and housed children from birth to three years old. We boarded an old, large, white van that spewed terrible exhaust fumes. Sergei was once again our driver but Michael stayed back in Moscow because his job was as a coordinator for families during the Moscow portion of their trip. Sergei helped us load the Little Tykes Cozy Coupe box, our suitcases of gifts and Barb and Loren's gifts into the back of the van.

We headed east out of Moscow to Vladimir, the main city and administrative center of the Vladimir Oblast or Region. We spent the three-hour van ride getting to know Loren and Barb and sharing our experiences. They told us that they chose not to tell ANYONE back home in Michigan where they were going so consequently, no one in their circle of friends and family knew they were adopting a baby that week in Russia. At the last minute, they confided in Loren's sister, in the event of an emergency. I found this nearly impossible to believe. Our story was the exact opposite and although they never said it, maybe they found our story as strange as we found theirs. I don't know.

The view outside the van window was even stranger to us. At that time, there were no suburbs surrounding the city of Moscow. The city limits abutted the endless forest. We abruptly went from an eleven-lane street in Moscow with its soviet-style apartment buildings to a two-lane bumpy road through the forest, where we would travel for the next three hours. There wasn't the gradual urban-suburban-rural transition we were accustomed to seeing in the United States.

There was nothing but flat land and miles and miles of dense forests filled with spruce, pine and oak trees. We rode for hours, just staring at those trees. Suddenly, in the middle of ABSOLUTELY nowhere in the forest, we came upon people on the side of the road, selling stuffed animals! Little ones and big ones, like those you'd win at a midway game at the Erie County Fair. The stuffed animals' bright colors stood in stark contrast to the white snow and dull, dark forest. We passed several of these makeshift roadside kiosks. Where did they come from and who exactly did they think would buy these stuffed animals? It was a fledgling attempt at free enterprise. I found it comical, awkward, confusing and profoundly sad at the same time.

We arrived in the city of Vladimir and stopped at the Adoption Center, a dark, two room trailer-like place. Tanya, a Russian woman, who was the EAC adoption coordinator for the Vladimir Region, met us there. After a twenty-minute wait, she joined us in the van and we all left to get our documents notarized. (There was always one more thing to do.) When we arrived at the notary office, Tanya took our passports and our travel visas. Outside the van, Tanya and Sergei were met by two other men. They all went inside and left Terry, Loren, Barb and me in the van with no money, no receipts, no passports and no travel visas. We were all a little leery but joked about being duped, a meager attempt to calm our nerves about the vulnerable situation in which we suddenly found ourselves.

Another guy came back to the van and announced he was coming with us. He was young and strikingly handsome with a thick mop of dark hair and brown eyes. He told us his name was Mikhail, that he was a Romanian Gypsy and worked as an EAC employee in Russia. When I was a child, I remember hearing frightening comments from my mother about gypsies "passing through town" in the summer, so this set me on edge and prejudiced my first impression of him. His English was superb and he promptly left to go buy a bouquet of flowers for the notary lady inside. Tanya appeared and returned our documents to us and announced she was not going with us to the Murom Infant Home to meet the babies. Sergei and Mikhail would take us.

We set off on the two-hour van ride to Murom. The landscape was flat and frozen; the endless forest continued. It was another clear, sunny, cold day. A few small villages that looked like progress had left them behind a century ago popped up along the way. Did they have running water? We could see smoke rising from the chimneys in the little stone cottages. We didn't ask any questions because we were busy absorbing what our eyes were seeing.

We continued on. The road was extremely bumpy and the van had no seat belts. At one point, we abruptly pulled over in the desolate forest and Mikhail got out. Terry and I didn't say a word, but our shared glance spoke volumes about our uncertainty. What was happening? Where was he going? Mikhail jumped-ran through the knee-deep snow and disappeared into the forest while we waited in frightened silence. We exhaled a sigh of relief when we realized it was merely nature calling. He got back in the van, wearing a sheepish grin and we were off again.

We arrived in the city of Murom a few hours later and picked up a lady whose job title was, "The Inspector." That's exactly what they called her. She was a government official and her role was as an advocate for the children.

Initially and naively, I thought the Russian government was valiant in appointing advocates for the children, but as the years went on, my thoughts on the government soured. I think a few words about the orphanage system are appropriate here.

At that time, Russia had the largest number of orphans in the world. We heard estimates of anywhere from six to seven hundred thousand children. A large percentage of them were not truly orphans, because they had at least one living parent. They were called "social orphans" and due to either poverty or neglect, parents abandoned them or had their parental rights taken away. Some parents were in prison. The Murom Infant Home, where Marissa lived, was considered a "Baby House." Baby Houses raised children from birth to three years old. The children who reached three years old and were not adopted, were taken away from their lifelong, familiar caregivers in the Baby Houses and sent to an orphanage for older children, where they lived until they reached fifteen. My subsequent research revealed that each year, two thousand children died in the orphanages. I don't know the causes of these deaths but I can only assume it was due to neglect, malnutrition and lack of medical attention.

Our Russian coordinators told us that when the children reached fifteen, they "graduated" from the system. They were given a little money, an outfit to wear and released into the world, despite having received an inadequate education or job training and having acquired few life skills training. Through many discussions with the Russian coordinators we met over the five years, we learned that once released from the orphanage system, many of the orphans turned to drugs, prostitution and other illegal activities like criminal gangs to survive. We also learned that the vast majority ended up either in prison, on the streets, or dead. The State was the only "parent" they ever knew. Only one in ten orphans went on to live a "normal" life.[7]

Years later, when I asked a Russian coordinator named Irina what would've happened to Madeline (our second daughter) if she wasn't adopted, her response was a curt, "You don't want to know." We have no way of knowing what the situation is today with the Russian orphanage system. Vladimir Putin banned Americans from adopting children from Russia in 2012. The Russian government provides no current information other than "now many Russian families adopt children." I've also read they instituted a foster care system in the country. Personally, I just don't trust this information.[8] Now back to my story about Marissa.

At one o'clock in the afternoon, we arrived at the Murom Infant Home, a two-story concrete building with old windows and hanging icicles. The backyard looked like a scene from a black and white, depression-era TV show.

Terry and I held hands and went inside. The smell of cooked cabbage hit our noses and that, coupled with my anxiety and the warm temperature inside, made me nauseous. We waited in a large empty room alone while the couple from Michigan were waiting for their son in another room, privately as well. On the wall of our room, someone had painted a colorful mural depicting a dancing bear and wolf along with other forest creatures. It was freezing outside, yet stiflingly hot inside, an open screenless window providing a little relief. The room was lined with little empty chairs all pushed together and contained a glass curio cabinet, filled with several old-fashioned toys on display. No child could possibly reach those toys. We were finally going to meet our baby! I can remember my breathing turned shallow and I had butterflies in my stomach.

At last, a woman walked in wearing an old fashioned white nurse's outfit and a white cloth surgical mask over her face. She was holding a baby, who was wearing a light green outfit and sweater. Her back was turned toward us. The woman turned the baby around and, for the first time ever, we saw our daughter's face.

She was a beautiful baby with blue eyes, white porcelain skin and a serious but curious gaze. Terry and I laughed out loud and cried as we took turns holding the baby and taking pictures. From the very first instant I held her, it felt right. "At last," I thought. It was the most incredible moment of our lives. We immediately felt such abundant feelings of love, belonging and family wash over us and flood our hearts and minds.

We spent half an hour alone with Marissa, passing her back and forth between us, kissing her and taking pictures. She was smiling and looking at each of us, as if to say, "What took you two so long?" She was so alert and robust. We didn't expect her to be so healthy looking. I remember that as I held her during that first meeting, my mind's eye looked toward our house in Orchard Park.

I whispered in her ear, "We are so far from home. We have to go. Everyone is waiting for you." I yearned to be back in her sweet, cozy nursery at home with her, where she belonged. To this day, I've never felt further from home than at that moment.

An orphanage worker came back into the room and told us it was time to go feed Marissa. We asked if we were allowed to see the room where Marissa slept each night so she led us to a small, dark and cold room with six small old-fashioned wooden cribs that lined the walls. Her crib was labeled Number Ten and was on the right side of the room, under a hand painted mural of two bunnies playing ball. The worker gave me a small silver cross that was hanging on her crib and told me Marissa had been baptized and this cross was hers. I silently wept when I saw where she slept, thinking of her many nights alone, when no one came to comfort her. They later gave me a written schedule of Marissa's day, which revealed that she spent approximately twenty-two lonely hours per day in that little crib.

We then went into a large, bright room that was well-lit from the numerous windows on the side. Again, cabinets with glass doors displayed old-fashioned toys perfectly and neatly lined up behind the glass, seemingly never touched by a child.

The center of the room was filled with a huge playpen that had colorful mobiles overhead and it held approximately ten babies, all about Marissa's age, identically dressed, lying on their backs. None of the babies were wearing diapers and each outfit was wet. I remember there being no sound. The babies didn't cry or fuss. They had learned long ago that their cries would often go unanswered. It was an eerie feeling, seeing so many babies and hearing only silence, the language of those lacking a mother's love.

The workers at the orphanage were caring and loving, but there were far too few of them to meet the needs of that many babies. We were told the orphanages were overcrowded and underfunded and we saw this first-hand. They didn't have money for diapers. I was completely overwhelmed and could not bear to look at all those babies.

This one particular woman named Gara, who appeared to have a strong emotional connection with Marissa, wanted to show me how to feed her. Terry smiled and talked to all the babies, reporting to me later that one little guy had vomit in his ear from his neighbor in the playpen. I disassociated and focused only on Marissa. I assume it was a coping mechanism to shield myself from the overwhelming sight of those babies. Marissa drank from a glass bottle with a heavy rubber nipple with a widened opening pulled over the top. It contained some watery brown gruel which was definitely not baby formula.

Terry joined me as Gara fed Marissa a bowl of porridge with vegetables. Through Mikhail's translation, Gara said Marissa's daily diet consisted of pureed vegetables, fish, poultry and eggs. That information was incredible to hear. No one I knew in the United States would feed that to an infant. Years later, people would comment that our kids would eat anything, as if they had adult palettes. Onions, garlic, fish, spinach, seafood, it didn't matter, they ate all of that as toddlers. Was it because they were exposed to such flavors at such a young age?

I continued to feed Marissa and then burped her. She vomited over my shoulder, all down the back of the only sweater I had with me. So much for wearing that every day. Again through Mikhail's translation, the women there said Marissa looked like us and said they thought we would be good parents. They were so happy for us. We placed Marissa in a walker, played with her some more and took more pictures. I cried most of the time we were in that room. The final release of the months of stress and worry must have caused that. At one point, I excused myself to use the restroom which was a tiled room with a simple hole in the floor.

Meanwhile, Sergei and Mikhail carried the majority of our gifts inside. They opened our boxes and suitcases and sorted through the items we brought. We later realized, not everything was destined for the orphanage. Some of the items would be distributed to officials, judges and government employees.

Mikhail came into the orphanage day room where we were and announced that Terry and I had to leave with him. We didn't want to leave Marissa, but he said we must and it was for the best. What was he talking about? We had just met our baby.

We hadn't had anything to eat or drink all day and the afternoon was getting late. We left the orphanage and went to a Russian restaurant that was very dark inside. Loren, Barb, Mikhail, Sergei, Terry and I all piled into a booth completely surrounded by a heavy red velvet curtain. Thick cigarette smoke and our anxiety hung in the air. A waiter pulled back the curtain and took our orders. Mikhail asked us if we wanted to adopt the babies and we all said yes, of course. The meal came and all I remember is that the food was very unusual. I ended up with clear soup with hotdog slices floating in it. Terry and I laughed at that. My upset stomach once again didn't allow me to eat much. The unusual food, the cigarette smoke choking our throats, the heavy curtain cocooning our booth and the overwhelming desire to go back to Marissa made me hot, anxious and nauseous. We finally left and went to buy candy and champagne for the workers at the orphanage. By then, it was four o'clock in the afternoon and due to the northern latitude and the time of the year, it was already dark outside.

We went back to the orphanage and spoke with the director who told us about Marissa's vaccinations. She led us into the room where Marissa was sleeping. The room was pitch black dark and there was Marissa, lying in her crib, on her back, wide awake. She was just lying there quietly, looking at the ceiling. It struck me as so pathetic and sad, causing me again to weep. She was wrapped so tightly in a yellowed sheet that she couldn't move anything but her head, which she shook back and forth. She was just waiting. We later realized the long days in that crib, staring at the door, waiting for someone to enter, caused the back of her head to be flat on one side.

Gara took Marissa out of her crib and led us into the washroom where there was a little hand towel hanging on a hook labeled "Rusheva Olga, #10." Gara splashed water on Marissa's face and bottom and Marissa just smiled. I changed Marissa into the pink, cozy outfit we brought from home. She would leave the orphanage with nothing but the silver cross from her crib, her papers and our love and hope for a wonderful life together.

Once she was ready and we were waiting for the director to complete some paperwork, Terry sat and held Marissa on his lap when one of the most beautiful things happened.

Gara knelt down before Terry and she took Marissa's tiny baby hands into her own and kissed each of them quietly and repeatedly. This lovely woman was sad to see Marissa go and through her tears, she said in English, "Farewell. Farewell."

Mikhail then translated her words "I know she will have a good life." This woman knew she would never see Marissa again and the finality of the goodbye was profound. Of course, I cried again as Terry and I hugged Gara and thanked her for taking care of our baby for us.

The orphanage system was an imperfect solution to a systemic, societal problem, but this noble woman did her best and her love for the children was abundantly clear. The orphanage just didn't have the resources they needed. That day, they told us that the women working there hadn't received paychecks in over a month and a half, yet they all still came every day to care for the babies.

We thanked Gara and the other workers and said goodbye. We then walked out into the dark and into the rest of our lives as a family.

Sergei and Mikhail got in the front seats, Barb, Loren and their baby Lucas took the second row while Terry, Marissa and I headed into the back row of the van. No seat belts also meant no car seats, so baby Marissa sat on Terry's lap tightly gripping one of his fingers with her right hand and one of my fingers with her left hand. She kept turning her head, taking turns looking up into each of our faces. She was calm, quiet and content. Knowing her personality now, I realize she was trying to observe, taking in her new surroundings and figuring out what was happening to her. She has always been an "old soul" and usually observed things most kids her age never bothered to notice.

I don't know if Marissa was tired, but she never closed her eyes for a second on that two-hour ride in the dark as we headed back to the city of Vladimir on the long and bumpy road through the frozen Russian countryside. We shared a special and very memorable experience in that van and we had a feeling of family like we never knew before.

Terry whispered, "It's amazing. She is OUR baby and it doesn't matter at all that she is adopted." We had so much love in our hearts for her. I cried silently and Mikhail turned around and jokingly asked if I was STILL crying. I told him it was a dream come true. We waited four years for Marissa. I felt like all of my humanity was on full display that day.

Chapter SIX

Once we arrived in Vladimir, our first stop was a Soviet-style apartment building where we parted ways with Loren and Barb. Terry, Marissa and I were led upstairs by Mikhail and Sergei. We would be staying with a "host family" for two nights. EAC told us this before we left home and I hated the idea. Why a host family? We never received an explanation for that question. It was uncomfortable, awkward, and too intimate. It was such a stressful time and I yearned for our privacy. We would've much preferred staying in a hotel room by ourselves.

Looking back on it, I suppose it was a way for the Russian coordinators to put money in the pockets of their friends. We paid the host family cash to stay with them. It was late in the evening, we were tired and overwhelmed and had a new baby with us. We were hardly in the position to engage in small talk with strangers.

After we were briefly introduced to our host family, Mikhail and Sergei left us. The family was wonderful and consisted of a father, mother, two teenage daughters, a grandmother and a large dog. I think they may have also had a son, but I can't remember clearly. But first, I have to describe the apartment that these people lived in.

It was on maybe the fourth or fifth floor of the old Soviet-style apartment building. The elevator was tiny, cramped and padded with a red vinyl cushion on the walls. It must have been acting as insulation for the cold. The hallway was narrow and concrete. The apartment door was also padded. The apartment was tiny and had a narrow hallway with a small kitchen to the immediate right. In the kitchen, they had a miniature banquette made of red vinyl and a small, low Formica table. The set was suitable for about four toddlers. There was a portable TV on the counter, and *Charles in Charge*, a decade-old American sitcom starring Scott Baio was playing, dubbed over in Russian. There was an apartment-sized refrigerator and a dog bowl on an elevated stand.

The living room down the hallway two steps to the right had a cardboard folding door with fake windows. In the room, there was a big entertainment center, an upholstered couch and matching chair. This is where Terry, Marissa and I slept.

One step further down the hallway was a bedroom on the right and a bedroom on the left. The one bedroom, where the parents slept, was so small that there was only room for a double bed. The door couldn't close because the bed was in the way; it took up the entire room. The other bedroom had a twin bed and a pull out chair. It was for their teenage children.

At the end of the hallway, a half step away were two doors. The one on the left was the water closet. It was so small, you couldn't sit on the toilet without your knees pressing against the cardboard door, which was covered in contact paper with a wooden design. The next room contained a sink and a bathtub that was piled TO THE CEILING with household sundries and supplies. This served as their broom closet, pantry, powder room, linen closet, utility room and coat closet. We weren't sure if they emptied the tub out once a week or if they bathed elsewhere.

Terry and I got Marissa settled in the living room and then the family's daughter, the only one who knew limited English, lightly knocked on the cardboard door, and told us our dinner was ready. She held Marissa while Terry and I sat, crouched at the low table with our knees pulled up to our chests. The daughter, along with her father and her sister stood around and watched us eat. They served us salmon, sausage, vegetables and a huge portion of mashed potatoes. I picked at my food and Terry, of course, ate heartily. We were both stressed, but he handled it better than I did. He could eat and sleep well even in this situation. His adaptability has served us well over the years while raising children together.

While we ate, they asked us a lot of questions about the United States and we, in turn, learned about their lives. They were warm, friendly people. The father was a civil engineer and had been to Boston on business. We paid them two hundred dollars in new U.S. currency to stay for the two nights and he said it was more than his salary for the month. To lend some perspective, according to Forbes, the minimum wage in Russia in 2020 is the equivalent to one hundred and sixty U.S. dollars per month. The fee we paid was very welcomed by the family and they told us that the grandmother and mother moved out of the apartment for a few days, making room for Terry, Marissa and me.

Marissa slept the whole night without making a peep on the pull-out chair, which served as a makeshift crib. I cringe now, thinking of how unsafe that was, having a five-month old baby risking suffocation while sleeping on a plush, soft chair, covered in a blanket. Terry and I slept on the nearby pull-out couch. I didn't wake once in the night either, which is surprising to me, given my anxiety level.

In the morning, Sergei and Mikhail picked us up to go get Marissa's passport picture taken. At the photo studio, Sergei sat in a chair and the photographer put a white sheet over his head and body. Then we handed him Marissa and he held her as they snapped her official photo. We laughed at this because we didn't realize that was how they photographed infants.

Marissa fell asleep on the way back to the apartment. I was still so anxiety-ridden and existing on water and pink Pepto-Bismol pills. All the driving on bumpy roads with an infant on my lap didn't help matters either. That afternoon, it was time to go to court to legally adopt Marissa. We unpacked our business attire, which, after being stuffed in a garment bag for three days, checked in an airplane for ten hours and tossed in a bumpy dirty van was not the best look we could've had. It would have to make do. We had no access to a shower or bath. You can imagine how we looked. We were instructed to leave Marissa with the host family, who would babysit her. Of course, we were very reluctant; we just met the host family the evening before! We felt so protective of Marissa. To convince us, Mikhail was forced to explain that legally, she shouldn't have left the orphanage with us the day before. This is the legal sequence of events of what SHOULD have taken place: first, we drive out to Murom to meet Marissa; second, we drive two hours back to Vladimir to go to court; third, we drive back to Murom to pick her up; and finally, we drive back to Vladimir to go to Vital Statistics and Immigration. Mikhail wanted to save time and eliminate some of that driving, so he and Tanya worked something out with the orphanage director and we were allowed to take her with us at our initial meeting. I think that's why we left the orphanage to go to lunch and why he brought champagne and candy for the orphanage director. We also assumed some of our new sequentially-number U.S. currency exchanged hands.

Court was a memorable and smooth experience. It was very cold outside and the sun was shining brilliantly. It was cold inside the old, worn down courthouse, but our hearts were warm and our spirits were soaring. The judge was a woman who wore a fur coat on the bench. The inspector and a prosecutor were there and they smiled at us and asked us many questions about how we would take care of Marissa. The judge left the courtroom and came back a moment later and said in Russian that we were now her parents. Terry and I hugged each other as I cried with relief. It was now official; Marissa was ours. What an incredible feeling that was. We felt some sense of security and permanency for the first time since we started the whole process.

We went back to the apartment and spent the rest of the day and night in our host family's living room, getting to know Marissa. Whatever that porridge was they fed her the day before at the orphanage did not agree with her little system. We thought maybe they fed her the porridge to impress us and that it wasn't something in her usual diet. We put her on a diet of baby formula we brought from home which was so infused with iron and nutrients that perhaps that is what caused her the nagging intestinal problems she was experiencing.

That evening, we were reflecting on our experience in court and we wondered if the woman judge was the recipient of the large ladies bathrobe, the bottles of scotch or the Cross pen and pencil set! We assumed the prosecutor, the inspector and others received some gifts as well.

The next day, we said our goodbyes to our host family. Their food nourished Terry's body and their kindness nourished both of our souls. Their tiny, cramped apartment was filled with an abundance of warmth and love. They wished us well and promised to try and stay in touch. We gave them our address in the U.S., telling them to write to us in the future. We never heard from them again.

Chapter SEVEN

We drove back to Moscow. Barb, Loren and Lucas joined us in the van. By now, we were getting more familiar with Sergei and Mikhail and we started to relax. Mikhail had a very engaging personality and he asked Terry to hand up his black "fur" hat he brought from home. Sergei, while driving, took out his cigarette lighter and tried to burn a small piece of the hat. The two of them laughed in the front seat and said Terry's hat wasn't a real *shapka*. Terry didn't care. That hat from Lina's Border Patrol days was warm!

On the ride, Mikhail had a lot of questions about the United States, and he told us he was trying to make his way over there in the near future. Months after we returned home to Orchard Park, Mikhail called us asking for Terry's help in immigrating. Terry explained that wasn't the type of law he practiced and referred him to someone else. I don't know about Terry, but I felt very unsettled, knowing the Russian coordinators could reach us, and therefore, Marissa in the United States so easily.

That day, when we arrived back in Moscow, we were supposed to go to the American Embassy, but because it was Thanksgiving Day, it was closed. It was the one and only place in the entire country that was closed and it was the one and only place we needed to go. In the end, it turned out to be such a memorable day, though. We settled back into the Hotel Ukraina. I bathed Marissa and discovered she had dark blond hair. Up until then, we thought it was dark brown. We realized that in the orphanage, her hair hadn't been washed with shampoo.

After her bath, Terry walked Marissa up and down the hallways of the hotel in her little stroller. She loved it. He came back and told me what he saw. There was a small bar on each floor of the huge, mostly empty hotel. Each bar was fully stocked with alcohol and had nightclub-like lights flashing. There was loud techno music playing and a bartender, clad in a white shirt and black tie, stood behind each bar. BUT THERE WERE NO CUSTOMERS IN ANY OF THE BARS. Not a single one. We thought it was so strange. Terry's walks with Marissa on the empty floors reminded me of the movie *The Shining*.

Someone told us there was an American Pizza Hut franchise in Moscow and gave us the phone number. We called but it was no longer Pizza Hut but a locally-owned small pizzeria. There were no other options for us that evening. We ordered pizza and when it arrived, I tipped the delivery man what I thought was an appropriate amount. I didn't understand the ruble exchange rate and we figured out later that I tipped the poor guy the equivalent of seventeen U.S. cents. I felt awful.

Barb, Loren and Lucas came to our room and we ate the pizza and the guys went and got us each a beer from one of the bars, while the babies played on the floor. My mother wisely advised me to pack a clean sheet from home for that very purpose. That whole day, the news on TV was consumed with the Chilean dictator, Augusto Pinochet. Although we had never heard of him before, it was big international news. I remember feeling like we had been living in our American "bubble," only concerned with matters of the United States. Up until that point in our lives, we were completely oblivious to news happening in other foreign countries. With the internet and the 24 hour news cycle, that is unimaginable today.

Barb and Loren left and we called our mothers, who were both so excited and surprised to hear from us. Those phone calls home were incredible. It was Thursday by now and no one had heard from us since we left Buffalo the Saturday before. When we called home, it was late morning in the U.S. and both of our mothers were beginning to prepare their huge family Thanksgiving meals. Just talking to them brought pangs of homesickness because we longed to be there, in those familiar surroundings on that special family holiday with Marissa.

When my mom answered the phone, I had such a lump in my throat and initially, all I could squeak out was a quiet, "We got her." My mom shouted to my father and we both cried happy, relieved tears.

That night, Terry placed Marissa on his chest in bed, where she was so content. Up until that point, she slept alone in her orphanage crib and this was the first time she slept with someone. He tried to put her down once she was asleep but she wanted NOTHING to do with her little portable crib again. She had us wrapped around her baby finger!

Friday morning, we teamed up with Michael, our Moscow coordinator again and Sergei, who drove us to the U.S. embassy. As we waited outside the Embassy, I decided to capture the moment with my camera and quickly was scolded by an armed guard that no photos were allowed. Once inside, it was a smooth process and we were there for two hours. The waiting room was crowded and noisy with American families adopting children. Everyone was talking to each other, sharing adoption stories and offering one another well wishes. It was so festive and uplifting to see all the families with their new children. Some people had older children they were adopting but most, like us, had infants and toddlers. It was incredible to see the parent-child bonds that already formed in the short time period they were together. The look of hope, trust, love and the promise of a bright future was on everyone's faces. When it was our turn, we had a quick interview with the Embassy employee and Marissa was cleared to come to the United States. Pride in being Americans swelled in our hearts.

Afterwards, we all went to McDonald's. There were four U.S. couples, the babies and a Russian coordinator in our group. While we ate, Marissa sat in a highchair and watched us take each mouthful. She was hungry, but we had her on a formula-only diet at that point. It was a relief for me to be able to eat a little and that familiar McDonald's cheeseburger tasted good.

We went back to the hotel to enjoy the baby and pack for our return flight to the U.S. the next day. I took Marissa's picture waving a little American flag we received at the embassy.

The next morning, Sergei dropped us off at the Moscow airport. We thanked him and said goodbye. We were traveling much lighter on this flight. So much had happened in the six days since we arrived in that same airport the Saturday before. We weren't as nervous; we had our baby and we were so excited and happy to be going home.

At that time, in 1998, there were no security check points in American airports but Moscow was different. We had four security checkpoints to go through, all guarded by members of the Russian military, bearing machine guns.

At each checkpoint, they looked at our U.S. passports and Marissa's Russian passport and put a little sticker on either the booklet itself or on an inside page. This experience was totally new to us. When we traveled after 9/11 in the U.S. with its newly-implemented airport security, it reminded me of that day.

The flight home was wonderful. It was a "baby flight," packed with families and their newly-adopted kids. The chaos and noise that accompanies traveling with kids filled the cabin. We were delirious with joy! We sat back in two coach seats and Marissa took turns sitting on each of our laps. She ate, slept and played, making the ten-and-a-half-hour flight pass quickly. What a great feeling it was when we landed in the United States at JFK airport. We'd only been gone one week, but the experience felt like a much longer adventure.

My childhood friend Kelly, who lived close by with her family, met us after we cleared customs. She came running up to us, crying and hugging us. It was such a relief to see her. I started crying and I remember thinking it was so surreal that we actually had a baby of our own. We got in their car and she, her husband Tom and their two boys drove us over to LaGuardia Airport for our flight to Buffalo. We had a glass of wine and told them all about our experience in Russia. They waited with us for a few hours until our Buffalo flight was ready to depart. Marissa just went with the flow. Nothing fazed her. She didn't cry or fuss. Like she was on the trans-Atlantic flight, she seemed to be enjoying the new experiences, interested and observing the things around her.

The flight to Buffalo felt like it was fifteen minutes long. Perhaps we dozed off; I don't know. By then, we were exhausted. When we were taxiing on the runway in Buffalo, I once again began to cry. My adrenaline and nerves caused me to shake. We were so exhilarated, yet so tired and drained. Our long journey was finally coming to an end.

As we pulled up to the terminal, we could see camera flash bulbs going off inside. We weren't sure who was there to greet us, but they were taking pictures of our plane. My emotions overwhelmed me as we walked off the plane and in those pre-9/11 days, people could walk right to the gate. I heard my sister Peggy yell, "Here they come!"

Terry carried the baby and into the airport we walked. We were greeted by over fifty people, family and friends alike, carrying balloons, waving flags, holding welcome banners and gifts. Camera flashes were going off and everyone was shouting, crying, cheering and clapping. It was an incredible moment and one that none of us had ever experienced before. Strangers stopped to join in the celebration and some of them were even crying tears of joy for us. We lingered at the airport gate for well over an hour as other friends and family continued to arrive and enjoy the homecoming. Everyone was greeting Marissa, passing her around, congratulating us and snapping pictures. She simply looked at everyone and never made a sound. It was one of the most exhilarating things I've ever experienced. Truly, a key scene in the highlight reel of our lives.

Chapter EIGHT

Finally, it was time to leave the airport for home. Our parents and some of our siblings came to our house with us. Outside, there were banners and balloons hanging from the house, the mailbox and the trees. Inside, there were balloons, flowers and gifts. We opened champagne and had a toast.

It was well past midnight when everyone finally left and Terry and I took Marissa up to her nursery for the first time. For some reason, all three of us slept on the floor of her nursery. I guess it was because we didn't want to leave her alone and she wanted no part of being alone in her new crib. By that time, Terry and I had been awake for close to thirty hours. We were completely wiped out and I silently cried myself to sleep. I don't cry easily or often but that particular week had been something else. I cried more that week than I ever have in my entire life! We were so happy to be finally home. It was November 28, 1998.

The next day brought a whirlwind of visitors. Marissa was reveling in all the attention. She just looked at everyone with a curious and steady gaze, unflappable with the new people and unfamiliar sights, smells and sounds. Of course, she had never heard the English language before, but she appeared to understand the language of love, attention and family.

On Monday, Terry and I took her to the pediatrician who gave her a clean bill of health. The weather was mild for the end of November and the three of us took a walk that evening. For over a year, Terry and I had lived in that house and never once had either of us walked down the street. All we ever did was drive up after work, pull into the attached garage and drive out the next morning to work again. For the first time, neighbors saw us, on a Monday evening, strolling down the street with a new baby in a stroller. I realized in that moment that my life had suddenly and completely changed forever.

Because it was a mild stretch of weather and because she had spent little or no time outside during her whole life, someone (I can't remember who) suggested I let Marissa take her nap in the stroller on the back porch. I bundled her up and did just that. I sat in the kitchen, writing thank you notes, keeping an eye on her in her stroller, mere steps away through the sliding glass doors.

Years later, my next door neighbor Kerri, whom I hadn't even met in the year we'd live there, would tell me a funny story. She was on the phone with her mother and looked out and saw a baby napping on our porch. She said to her mom, "That girl next door didn't look pregnant and now she has a baby outside on her porch! Where do you think the baby came from?" We didn't know it then, but in the coming years, we'd grow very close and we would raise our kids together.

That winter, Marissa enjoyed her first Christmas and we had her baptized in the Catholic church. Although the Russians told us she was baptized, we had no paperwork proving that to be true, so we baptized her in the United States.

She adjusted well to life with us. However, there were small signs that reminded us of her origin story. She was home with us for three months before we could get her to laugh. She was always smiling but quiet. One day in February, Terry called me downstairs.

"Come quick," he yelled. "Marissa is laughing!"

He put her stuffed brown bear on his head and for the first time, she laughed out loud.

When we adopted Marissa, we signed a contract with EAC, stating that we would provide a post-placement report for the Russian government once a month for our first year with Marissa. In addition, we had to have a social worker visit our house four times over the next three years and submit reports to the Russian government after each visit. We dutifully complied with these requirements.

It was amazing to see the power of love in action. Marissa grew and developed and began to hit all the milestones, some even early. She walked at ten months old and began to talk at the same time. She loved her first trip to Florida with us and our extended family in April. We celebrated her first birthday in June and had a great summer at the cottage. She adored her cousins and had a wonderful time on the beach, in the lake and on the rowboat.

In July, we received a letter from the U.S. Department of Justice, inviting us to a special citizenship ceremony they were hosting at the Buffalo Zoo on July 28, 1999. We, along with our entire families, attended as Marissa officially became a United States citizen. The day was beautiful, sunny, warm and cloudless and it was very moving to see and hear the large crowd assembled say the Pledge of Allegiance and sing the national anthem. Close to seventy internationally-adopted children became citizens that day. We knew a few of them from our parenting class and would come to know a few more who lived in Orchard Park. Two of the children ended up in Marissa's class at school.

We had a big celebration with about eighty people under a backyard tent at the cottage after the ceremony. The party went late into the evening, long after Marissa was put to sleep in her crib. We all wore red, white and blue and everyone felt extreme pride in the United States. Marissa received a congratulatory letter from President Bill Clinton and Aunt Moe and Uncle Jim gave her a very special gift. They arranged to have a United States flag flown in her honor over the U.S. Capitol Building in Washington, DC that day. We received the flag as a keepsake a few weeks later in the mail. They would eventually do this for all three of our girls, providing each of them with that special keepsake.

I was enjoying my time at home with Marissa. Bell Atlantic, then re-named Verizon, treated me generously and fairly. They paid us five thousand dollars toward Marissa's adoption expenses, they held my job for the year and still gave us free phone service. When my leave of absence ended, I decided not to return full-time. They offered me a position, working two days a week from home and I took it and placed Marissa at a daycare facility in the village of Orchard Park.

Acting on the advice of EAC, our adoption agency, we re-adopted Marissa in Surrogate's Court in Erie County. Our parents attended and it was a nice occasion that offered a sense of finality to us, knowing we made the adoption legal in the United States and now, her American birth certificate would be on file in Albany, the capital of New York State.

Life for the three of us was idyllic, full of reading books, dinners together, walks outside, trips to the playground, carefree summers at the cottage, family vacations in Florida, playdates and field trips. It carried on like this, full of good health, love, joy and fun for another year when Terry and I felt another longing creep into our consciousness.

Chapter NINE

On September 7, 2000, I placed a call to EAC. Terry and I were ready for our second baby.

Two days later, I received the blank paperwork from EAC and we began our journey to adopt our precious Madeline Grace. We didn't know it at the time, but she was already two months old.

Since the paperwork was exactly the same, this time I found it easier to complete. And not working full time, meant I had more time to complete it. The Office of Vital Statistics in the City of Buffalo had digitized its records meaning we didn't have any issues with Terry's birth certificate this time.

The process wasn't new, so it didn't seem as overwhelming. Our Baker Victory home study, the foreign dossier and the Immigration paperwork were all completed without a hitch and Terry and I were placed on the EAC "Magic Wall" by October 27, 2000.

Interestingly, Baker Victory dropped the parenting class requirement. It seemed like our little class in 1998 was one of the first AND last classes they held. That was fine by us because Terry and I had two years parenting experience under our belts by then.

Everyone was so happy about the news of a second baby, including Marissa, who was excited about getting a sibling. She was convinced Santa Claus was the person responsible for this, which was better than her original idea that Terry and I could go to the grocery store and buy a new baby.

Marissa included her new sibling in her prayers every night. "Dear God, please keep our new baby safe and warm and cozy and please bring our baby home soon," she'd pray out loud. Now that I knew what life in the orphanage was like, thinking of our new baby there was extremely painful. In November, I called EAC and asked if we could adopt again from the Vladimir Region. We knew the people and the first experience had been so positive, despite it being harrowing and anxiety-laden. EAC called me back.

"Things have changed over in Russia," Claire said. "They are requiring two trips now. One trip to meet the baby and then a second trip to go back and adopt the baby," she explained.

I was so deflated. That information was very difficult to absorb. Last time, the trip was so quick. Now, we'd have to ask someone to care for Marissa for at least one week and then again when we got the "hurry up, you're leaving in five days" call for our second trip. This was a lot to ask of our families. It was a lot for Terry to juggle with his increasingly demanding job as a lawyer. It was a lot of traveling and both of us were definitely NOT excited about another stay at the Hotel Ukraina. Nevertheless, we were firm in our decision to go forward.

We waited for the call with a referral. Christmas came and still there was no call. I put gifts under the tree for the baby, knowing the baby was celebrating Christmas alone, over in Russia. We had a nice Christmas but we had an empty, aching feeling. I wrote the baby a letter that evening in the glow of the Christmas tree lights.

On Friday, January 5, 2001, at twelve-thirty in the afternoon, the phone rang and it was Cindy from EAC.

"We have a baby for you!" she exclaimed.

"We have a medical report and five photos of a beautiful baby girl. She is from Smolensk and was born June 7, 2000, and her name is Julia Aripenkova."

"If you don't go get this baby, I'm going to get her. She is just precious," Cindy joked.

I was so excited that I started to cry happy tears as Cindy placed me on hold to find out how far Smolensk is from Moscow. It turned out that Smolensk was a large city on the border of Belarus and we would be taking a six-hour train ride to get there. Again, I was so relieved that no Russian plane rides were in the plan.

The baby was seven months old and was very small for her age. She weighed just over four pounds at birth and now she weighed only eleven pounds. I called Terry at work and he was so excited, but he was very worried about her low weight.

Marissa was sitting on her potty chair when I told her the baby was a girl and she yelled, "Yeah, a baby girl! Not a baby boy!"

On Saturday afternoon, January 6, FedEx delivered her photos and the medical report. She was absolutely adorable but oh so small. The photos showed her lying on a crazily patterned sheet covered in pictures of bananas and other fruit.

We had concerns.

Through EAC, I discovered Dr. Ira Chasnoff, who headed up the Child Study Center in Chicago. He was a subject-matter expert on Russian adoptees, having studied over a thousand of them by then. For a one hundred and twenty-five dollar fee, he would read the medical report, view the photos and give prospective parents his opinion on the child's health and well-being. I thought this was a good idea so I sent him the baby's medical report and pictures. He called me the next day.

"First of all, don't believe the part about her laughing and babbling," he said, referring to the sentence in the medical report that stated the baby was doing those things in her orphanage.

"In all the babies I have seen, I have NEVER seen any of them laugh or babble," he continued. "That is a lie," he concluded.

"I would estimate that developmentally, she is the equivalent of a two- or three-month old," he stated. "What I am observing in the photos is severe neglect," he continued. "Other than that, I have no real concerns. You should go over to Russia and meet her and then you can decide."

This was very hard for us to digest. Go and decide? I decided the moment Cindy called me. In our hearts and minds, this little girl was already one hundred percent ours. Still, a few years of parenting and talks with other adoptive parents had taught us to become more pragmatic and less emotional in how we reacted to things.

I liked and trusted Dr. Chasnoff. We were also reassured because included in his price was his willingness to be available for a phone call from Russia, regardless of the time in Chicago. We could call him if we saw things that caused us concern.

He recommended we bring our video camera and take videos of the baby in the orphanage and send those along to him when we got home from meeting her.

The baby's medical report from the orphanage seemed strange to us because it didn't say much. It stated that the baby's state was of medium hardness (hardness? Not hardiness? What did harness mean?) due to "fetal hypoxy, neurological symtomathy" and that was all it said. Dr. Chasnoff indicated he had seen these particular diagnoses many times on the medical reports and they didn't translate into anything meaningful.

We accepted the referral on January 9, 2001, and began to prepare the nursery. I selected a soft green and yellow motif with wallpaper that looked like a flower garden bordering the whole room, along with coordinating custom window treatments. Her room looked like a page out of the Pottery Barn catalog and it was perfect. It was feminine, delicate and calming.

In the meantime, Terry and I wrote down dozens of girl's names we liked. We liked her Russian name, Julia, but didn't feel right about keeping it because we didn't keep Marissa's Russian name, Olga. We also didn't know the significance of their Russian names. Were the girls named by their birth mothers? The orphanage directors? The Minister of Education? There were simply too many unknowns, so we decided to select our own name for the baby.

Carly and Paige were in the running. We discussed the names while lying in bed one particular evening. I had loved the name Madeline since I met a girl by that name in high school. Her nickname would be Maddy, which I also loved. Terry agreed. He would go on to give her many nicknames over the years, but "Maddy Magoo" came on the scene early and stuck. I wanted Grace as her middle name because its meaning of "kindness and generosity" is so beautiful and the name flowed so well with Madeline. Madeline Grace Higgins it was, and I promptly ordered her little pink and white personalized notecards from Crane for the dozens of thank you notes I knew I'd soon be writing.

While awaiting word on a travel date, I had a special intention Mass said for Madeline at our parish, Nativity of Our Lord in Orchard Park. Terry, Marissa and I attended and we all prayed for our new baby, her health and her safety.

Chapter TEN

Two and a half weeks later, we got the call that we were leaving in five days. I quickly scrambled to send, via FedEx, all the necessary paperwork to the Russian Consulate and wait for our travel visas. I made arrangements for Marissa to stay at my sister Peggy's house, for the short trip. EAC explained that we would be following a whirlwind schedule on our first trip.

Here it is: first, we would fly to New York on Tuesday, January 30, and then to Moscow overnight, arriving in the morning of January 31. We'd spend the first day in a Moscow hotel, resting up. Then, that very same evening at eleven o'clock, we'd leave the hotel and board an overnight train out to Smolensk for a seven-hour ride. We would arrive in Smolensk in the morning of February 1, drive to the Krasny Bor Baby House and meet Madeline Grace. We would turn around immediately and board a high speed train that afternoon back to Moscow. We would spend one night in a Moscow hotel and fly back to New York the next morning. We would be home on Friday, February 2. The entire trip would only take four days. It was crazy, but we were ready to do it. We were told that after our trip, the Russian government would invite us back in two or four weeks to go to court to adopt the baby.

EAC abandoned the gift list and only gave us guidelines of what to bring. By 2001, American products were more readily available to the Russians. In addition, there were approximately four thousand Russian children adopted by Americans in 2001 alone.[9] These families were all traveling to Russia, bearing gifts. Our agency was only affiliated with a few regions in Russia and therefore, they were only arranging adoptions in a handful of orphanages. The Russians must have long exhausted their specific gift lists and would accept anything at that point.

Back to packing for our first trip to meet Madeline. We had six thousand dollars in cash for this trip and a six thousand five hundred-dollar certified check payable to a woman named Irina. They told us to bring three gifts for women and one gift for a man. Nothing for the children. Their suggestions included a leather purse or bag, an average-sized pair of men's dress pants and a men's sweater, French perfume such as Estee Lauder, a day planner and gloves, and a hat and scarf set for a woman. I purchased all those suggestions.

It was raining when Terry's parents drove us to the Buffalo airport Tuesday morning. As we were leaving, Marissa said "Give Madeline a kiss for me, Daddy."

The flight to New York was good and we found navigating the New York airport much easier this time. We packed significantly lighter because it was a short trip and we had far fewer gifts this time. We also didn't have any supplies for the baby, since we would be coming home without her. We were already familiar with the JFK shuttle system and we didn't arrive as early in the day this time around. Also, our stress level was lower this time because we thought we knew what to expect.

The flight to Moscow was nearly empty, so we were able to stretch out over several seats and sleep. What an unexpected luxury that was. While in New York, we met Sandra and Reggie from Alabama, who were adopting through EAC and traveling with us. Reggie had a son who was twenty years old from a previous relationship and they were going to adopt Luba, a two-and-a-half year old girl, who would be their first child together. They chose to keep her Russian name because it meant "love" and they liked that.

I was armed with our video camera, ready to take lots of video footage of Madeline to show Marissa, our families and Dr. Chasnoff. I also brought Holy Water someone gave us to bless the baby and a religious crib medal that I planned to leave for her.

When we landed in Moscow, it was thirty-six degrees outside and snowing. I was so much more relaxed this trip. Irina, our coordinator, met us at the airport. She was such a nice woman and her English was excellent. From the blue

Mitsubishi SUV we were driving in, we noticed some changes in Moscow. Every apartment building now had TV satellite dishes hanging off the balconies. Car dealerships had popped up and there were luxury-brand vehicles on the road, like Cadillac Escalades and Lincoln Navigators, evidence of the wealthy oligarchs who lived in Moscow. According to Forbes, Russia has ninety-nine billionaires today. This is the fifth-most of any country.

We were in for another unexpected treat. We were not staying at the old Hotel Ukraina. Instead, we stayed at the newly opened, beautiful, very Americanized Radisson Slavyanskaya Hotel and Business Center, which was on the Moscow River. The hotel had restaurants, a business center, a movie theater, a swimming pool and an underground shopping mall. A quick check on TripAdvisor today reveals that not much has changed since 2001; the current price for a one-night stay in a standard room is thirty U.S. dollars. The website shows the same bathroom, bed, headboard, furniture and carpet we had in our room back in 2001.

Once we checked into the Radisson Hotel, we once again had to relinquish our passports, but felt a bit more at ease with it being an American establishment. We got to our room and both slept very soundly for a few hours and then went to a late lunch/early dinner in the hotel lobby restaurant where we had "Radisson burgers" and French fries.

EAC had a hospitality suite and office in the hotel, which served as a gathering place for parents and a place to get answers to any questions we might have. We stopped in and saw Oksana, the girl who gave us the tour of Moscow two years earlier. We were so happy to see her. We hugged hello and told her how Marissa was doing. Margaret, the Executive Director of EAC, our agency in Ohio happened to be there, setting up the EAC office in the hotel. We had never met her before, so we enjoyed introducing ourselves and explaining we were adopting our second baby. She told us many families were "repeat" clients.

After, Terry and I went back to our hotel room for the evening while we waited for the eleven p.m. train departure. Suddenly, there was a knock at our hotel room door. We froze and were immediately on edge as we peered through the door's peephole. It was a hotel employee. What did he want? We decided to open the door and discovered it was the hotel manager bringing me a complimentary fruit basket and a bottle of wine. It was my thirty-sixth birthday that very day and I never even gave it a thought up until that moment! The hotel had possession of our passports and must have noticed my birthdate. What a memorable celebration we had. We enjoyed the wine, munched on some fruit and watched an episode of *Magnum, P.I.* on TV. It had the Russian language dubbed over the original English audio track, making it a little difficult to follow. That television show had been off the air in the United States for thirteen years by then and we laughed, thinking the Russians must have thought it was current. We were excited to go meet Madeline and were both very pleased with how the trip was progressing. At that time, we were not very adventurous travelers, so we relaxed and enjoyed some of the Western touches.

Soon, it was eleven o'clock in the evening on our first day in Russia, and it was time to check out of the hotel and leave. We gathered all of our luggage and Irina picked us and Sandra and Reggie up in the hotel lobby. We walked in the cold, dark night to the Kievsky Train Station, which was located next door. There are eight major railway train stations in Moscow and this was one of the busiest. We would be taking a night train out to Smolensk, Russia, which is two hundred and fifty miles west of Moscow, close to the border of Belarus.

The Kievsky Station was huge and cavernous and very surreal. I found it scary at that hour, like going back in time. It was so old-fashioned and the smell of burning oil or coal overwhelmed us. Once again, like in the Moscow airport, we heard a loud speaker, with a lady's voice. This time, it was echoing out in the cold night air, repeating something over and over. It was a very unsettling feeling. Terry and I both commented that it was like a scene in a movie.

The train ride turned out to be one of the most memorable of our Russian experiences. The outdoor platform had little or no lighting and we got on an old train that looked like something from World War I. I'm sure it was. It was a long distance passenger train with sleeping accommodations. These types of trains, we found out, are typically very slow-moving and they use older carriages.

We were in first class, which meant we had our own cozy little compartment with two very small berths, already made up with clean, crisp sheets, a pillow and a heavy woolen blanket. There was a small table between the berths that had a vase with artificial flowers in it. Above it, there was a window. Irina showed us to our sleeping compartment and told us to lock the door behind her and to ABSOLUTELY NOT open it for anyone, not even the train attendant under ANY circumstances. She warned us of train bandits who robbed passengers. She showed us how to wedge a piece of cardboard above the door so no one could break in. I was duly frightened by her remarks and actions, so Terry locked the door as instructed and we settled in for the night. Irina was riding on the train in her own compartment as were Sandra and Reggie. Irina told us she would knock on our door in the morning.

The walls to our compartment did not go all the way up to the ceiling and next to us, there were Russian comrades eating something that smelled like bologna. They drank, laughed, ate, talked and smoked cigarettes for most of the night.

The train lumbered along slowly and we looked out the window at the desolate forest scenery. Although it was dark, the white snow on the ground illuminated the forest. It snowed most of the night and it was one of the most adventurous experiences we had. We were going to meet our daughter! It was beautiful to watch out the window and the slow chug-chugging of the train was very soothing. Periodically we would stop for a minute or two at a small, remote, outdoor station and we'd once again hear a loud speaker with a woman's voice, ringing out into the night air. We both loved that night. I slept a little but Terry didn't at all. It was exciting and memorable to be traveling in such an unusual way to meet our baby. Over the years, we've often shared our memories of that special night.

Morning came and so did Irina. We were so excited to meet Madeline. I opened my carry-on to get my toothbrush and much to my dismay, my video camera had clicked on sometime during the travels and the battery was completely dead. There would be no videos to take. I almost cried but took a deep breath and carried on. We took turns visiting the bathroom down the corridor, which had nothing but a hole down onto the train track below. There was a samovar, heated by coal for hot water. This was indeed an old train.

Over a thousand years old, Smolensk is among the oldest of Russian cities. It holds a special place in the Russians' hearts because of its significant history. It is here that Napoleon entered Russia after a long-fought battle where thirty thousand men lost their lives.[10] Tolstoy wrote about it in *War and Peace*. Today, over three hundred and twenty thousand people live in the bustling city.

It was dark and cold when our train arrived in Smolensk at 6:40 a.m. A driver took all of us to the basement of a Russian hotel to eat breakfast, which consisted of a strange menu of cold corn and peas, liver, meats, mashed potatoes and a mixture of sour cream and cottage cheese. I didn't eat much. Because we couldn't read the signs, I mistakenly used the men's room and Terry used the women's bathroom. I had no memory of this hotel or breakfast, until I read my journal and then I remembered how we laughed at the bathroom gaffes.

The driver had a "homemade" limo, which was a blue decrepit Lada with little curtains hanging in the backseat windows. The driver played Euro dance pop music with a constant electric beat added to it. The songs all sounded the same; it played everywhere we heard music on that trip and got on our every last nerve.

We went over to the Ministry of Education, where Irina picked up our documents. We saw Madeline's picture on a computer screen and while she was adorable, she had a forlorn expression on her face, which we interpreted as communicating sadness or loneliness. That was when we found out her name, Julia, was pronounced *Yulia* and although that was a very pretty name, we were happy with our decision to name her Madeline Grace.

We were finally getting closer to meeting Madeline. I was growing anxious and impatient but then Irina announced that Terry and I had to go upstairs to have an important meeting with the Minister of Education in his office. What did he want? Was something wrong? All kinds of scenarios quickly raced through our minds while my stomach knotted up and my chest tightened with stress, fearing something had gone terribly wrong. Why didn't they ask to speak to the other American couple as well? I feared something had happened to Madeline. We entered to find that there was a translator in the man's office with us. Through the translator, the Minister of Education began to talk and proceeded to tell us jokes and talk about George Bush and New York City. He made racist remarks about black people and then spoke about the American education system. We couldn't believe this was happening. We literally traveled four thousand miles by trains, planes and automobiles and we were moments away from meeting our daughter and THIS guy wanted to shoot the breeze? As he continued to pontificate, we felt like we were stuck in quicksand or a bad dream where you try to run and can't.

After continuing to blather on for a while, he finally said, "Time is money and I am a busy man." The meeting was promptly over. His closing comment seemed to insinuate that WE were detaining HIM from something important. By the way, this busy man's desk was completely empty except for a magazine, a newspaper and a pack of cigarettes. Terry and I were shaking our heads when we got into the hallway, still unclear as to why we were summoned. The Russian government had a very bizarre way of conducting business.

Chapter ELEVEN

From there, we drove out to the Krasny Bor Baby House, Madeline's orphanage. Krasny Bor means "beautiful pine." We left the city center of Smolensk at ten o'clock in the morning and traveled on a two-lane road through the dense forest. Terry and I were quiet, lost in our own thoughts. He told me later that after driving for a while on the forest road, he said a silent prayer, "God, please give me a sign that this is the right thing to be doing" and IMMEDIATELY after that, we turned into a driveway.

Krasny Bor Baby House was set back off the road, deep in the woods, at the end of a winding, unplowed road. There were several buildings on the compound with old-fashioned baby carriages, strollers, bikes and teeter-totters strewn about the grounds, covered in snow. In front of the main building, there was an enormous dog, chained to a tree. They told us that during the last century, the smaller buildings were cottages or "dachas" for very rich people in Smolensk. It was now an orphanage that housed one hundred children from birth to three years old.

We went inside the old large main building, and were overwhelmed by the smell of cooked cabbage and stale hot air. The place was in a state of disrepair: paint was peeling and many floor tiles were missing. Nervous and excited, we waited in the medical director's office, while she chatted in Russian to Irina. I remember her as having a gold front tooth, something we didn't see often in the U.S.

While we were waiting to meet the children, Reggie and Sandra were off-handedly told that their two-year-old daughter, Luba was NOT at the orphanage, but that she was in a Smolensk hospital, recovering from spinal surgery. Maybe they were in shock or perhaps they were just remarkably composed people, but they handled that news with incredible aplomb. It was as if someone told them Luba was taking a bath in another room. Spinal surgery? Terry and I could NOT believe our ears and we exchanged a worried glance that said, "Oh yes, that's just a garden-variety procedure for a two-year-old to be having." Reggie and Sandra remained calm, cool and collected and since they weren't meeting their child, they stayed in the room and waited to meet Madeline with us. I didn't like being with a group of people, meeting our daughter. I much preferred the privacy we were afforded when we met Marissa.

Finally, an older woman with red hair came in, carrying a large bundle of quilts and blankets. The medical director took the bundle, unwrapped the top quilt and out popped Madeline!

She had a HUGE open-mouth smile, marking her dramatic entrance as if to shout, "Ta-Da! I'm here!" It reminded me of someone popping out of a cake. We were so surprised that Terry and I both started laughing. That first impression perfectly sums up Maddy's personality. Throughout her childhood and now, as a young adult, Madeline makes someone laugh every single day. She is the epitome of *joie de vivre.*

Madeline was dressed in a pink sweat suit, a white cotton bonnet and two layered pairs of socks that were way too large for her. Weeks later, when we came back to take her home, she was still wearing that same outfit. I realized then that the orphanage only had one outfit for each baby, which they wore daily.

She was adorable and so tiny. One week shy of nine months old, weighing only eleven pounds, she had two teeth, which served as a reminder that although she was the size of an infant, she was much older. She was unable to sit up and she didn't snuggle into us when we held her. She just folded into herself and flopped around. There was no muscle tone in her body. We took turns holding her and taking pictures. Based on advice from Dr. Chasnoff, we wanted to look the baby over entirely, looking for birthmarks, tumors, anything really, so we undressed her and she screamed and howled to the point where the medical director got very annoyed with us!

We found out Madeline's birth mother was a sixteen-year-old student and her birth grandmother had signed the adoption papers. Madeline had a shaky left eye and from endless hours in her crib, the cartilage of her ear was folded over. She had a rash on her cheeks, watery eyes and a stuffy nose, presumably all due to a cold or allergies. She also had three sacral dimples at the base of her spine, one quite deep.

We held and played with Maddy for a while and then the most remarkable thing happened. Terry laid Madeline on her back in his lap and he rubbed his nose to her nose and she laughed out loud, giggled and smiled. It was a wonderful sound to hear and music to our ears. We were not only surprised, but elated. Dr. Chasnoff in Chicago was wrong. The baby DID laugh and giggle. This was highly unusual behavior for a baby in an orphanage. Her resiliency brought tears to my eyes. This baby lived in near complete deprivation, was neglected beyond our comprehension, yet she knew how to laugh and smile. This trait still carries Maddy through the bumpiest parts of her life. She has a remarkable ability to see the bright spot in all things. I remember saying to someone later, when she was three years old, that, "Every day is sunny in Madeline world."

Madeline started getting tired and began to suck on her two fingers, not her thumb, but her two fingers, a habit she had developed in the orphanage. It ended up altering her soft palate, making the midline of her teeth off kilter. She was fitted with braces in first grade and that ended the finger sucking. But up until then, it was a habit I would welcome during her unusually active toddlerhood. Finger sucking meant she was tired and would soon be asleep, which meant that a much-needed break from her constant motion and mischief was on the horizon.

Soon, we were told it was time to leave Madeline and catch a train back to Moscow. Terry and I would go back to the United States the following day, without our baby. We felt so profoundly sad, leaving her. It's difficult to describe how awful we felt. She was OUR daughter and we were leaving her THERE, in that godforsaken place? What? We felt anger and confusion about the arbitrary rule of needing to take two trips. We felt anxious and nervous about her health and her ability to sustain herself until we came back. She was so small and frail. We were scared that something would go wrong, that we wouldn't be able to come back to get her; and worst of all, scared that someone from Russia would adopt her in the meantime. It was way beyond sadness. It was like a cruel joke. Terry and I never felt so overloaded with simultaneous negative emotions in our lives. I cried when we said goodbye and left a religious crib medal and a rattle for her. I told her we'd be back in a few weeks to take her home. It was dreadful.

We left the Krasny Bor Baby House and went to a hospital in Smolensk, so Reggie and Sandra could meet their daughter. When we arrived, they went inside while Terry and I waited in the car, alone. We couldn't believe our eyes. I would use one word to describe the exterior of that hospital, deplorable. It was an old building with old windows, some broken, some open in the cold air. People were coming and going in and out of the entrance, most of them smoking cigarettes. We sat for about twenty minutes alone in the car, repeating, "Do you believe this?" The driver was outside and he left the car running with that electro pop music playing. It was so agitating.

After they finished inside, Reggie and Sandra came back to the car. To our surprise, they were smiling. They told us they walked into the hospital and happened to stumble upon Luba, who was walking around the hall. They were completely nonplussed by the situation and again, we couldn't believe the grace and dignity they displayed. They were thrilled to see their daughter, who appeared to be healthy and happy. In my mind, I was thinking, *Who was watching her? A two- year-old child was unattended in a hospital, wandering around?* But I kept my thoughts to myself and, instead, we shared in their contagious enthusiasm.

Despite the winter weather, we all went to eat lunch at an outdoor kiosk near a park where I remember watching two cross-country skiers. It was here that I asked Irina what would happen to Madeline if we didn't adopt her. "You don't want to know," she said, and that was the end of the conversation.

After lunch, we caught a high-speed, modern train back to Moscow. Terry and I both slept on the train, arriving at seven o'clock that evening. The train station smelled like burning coal and it was very dark and cold outside. Back at the Radisson hotel, we enjoyed hot showers and a bottle of wine as we called home and spoke with our mothers about Madeline.

The next morning we took a flight back to New York. It was one of the "baby flights" I mentioned earlier. Many families were on the plane, bringing their babies home. The cacophony of babies crying, people talking and laughing, kids playing, jumping on seats and moving around, filled the cabin. It was like rubbing salt in a wound to us. We didn't have our baby and we were like two shell-shocked soldiers, unable to believe we had to leave her there alone, go home without her and come all the way back to Russia in a few weeks to finally pick her up.

Something happened on the plane, which survives as the funniest incident of the five collective trips we took to Russia. My emotional state was not right, to say the least; neither was Terry's. We were edgy, tensions were running high and we were filled with sadness.

As usual, there was a group of loud, laughing Russians near us. One guy, who was drinking vodka, yucking it up with his comrades, laughing, talking and having the time of his life, refused to sit down. He seemed to know people seated in front of us, behind us and across from us. Terry had an aisle seat in the middle section of the large plane. While the Russian guy was talking to his friends, he was leaning his raised arms on the overhead compartment, right over Terry's head. The man either hadn't showered in a few days or he wasn't a deodorant user and the smell of body odor wafting from his armpits into Terry's face was unbearable. Terry and I rudely covered our noses with our shirts, making *ugh* noises loudly. Terry kept saying to me, "Do you believe this guy?"

A flight attendant came by, pushing a beverage cart and she needed to get past the man. Instead of sitting down, in an effort to give the flight attendant enough space to pass by, he turned around and leaned his rear end RIGHT into Terry's face. Terry lost it. He hauled off and punched the man right in the back of the thigh and shouted, "SIT DOWN!" Everyone looked at us, stunned. The man did sit down and he never got back up again.

I started laughing so hard at the absurdity of it all that my shoulders were shaking up and down. Terry, still fuming, kept looking at me saying, "What? Why are you laughing? That guy's an asshole. He stinks! His ass was in my face!" I would calm down after a while and then later, think of the incident once more and start laughing all over again. It was just like trying not to laugh in church.

The poor Russian man sitting next to me was reading his book and kept his elbows hugged tightly to his sides for the whole ride. Obviously, he understood English and heard all the rude things we were saying. Maybe he was aware of his own possible body odor and didn't want to be on the receiving end of a punch.

Eventually, Terry joined me in the laughter because he realized how ridiculous it all was. But that didn't last for long. When we were landing in New York, the flight attendant gave the usual instructions for everyone to put their tray tables up and their seats in the upright locked position. Apparently, the person in front of me didn't put his seat in the upright position quickly enough for Terry. Terry reached in front of me and hit the back of the guy's seat with his open palm, yelling at him, "Put your seat up, for crissake." I was laughing uncontrollably now. This behavior was completely out of character for Terry. He was nutty on that flight and I didn't even know who he was. The Terry I knew was a gentle, kind and unflappable person, but everyone has a limit, I suppose. I've heard the oft-told story of toddler Terry taking his shirt off in a restaurant when his food didn't arrive quickly enough. This was the same type of situation for him, apparently. The whole thing was ridiculously funny and crazy. I think Terry's out of control behavior was a manifestation of the hurt, frustration and fear he felt about leaving Madeline in Russia.

Chapter TWELVE

When we returned home, it was wonderful to see Marissa and tell her all about her baby sister. Everyone in our circle of family and friends was interested in hearing about the new baby, too. I sent the photos we took and the notes we wrote about Madeline to Dr. Chasnoff in Chicago. He called and said that after studying over a thousand adopted Russian orphans, his professional opinion was that Madeline was equivalent to a three-month-old baby, developmentally and physically. He thought she "looked good" and that she would rebound once she was at home. He observed that she appeared to be a child that had been very neglected.

I also sent Madeline's medical report and my notes to a local pediatrician, who shall remain nameless. He called me and said, "I have concerns. She doesn't look good. You could be inviting problems into your life. This isn't like buying a new car. You already have one healthy child, you should be happy with that."

I was so stunned and upset by his abrupt, dismissive and uncaring words. This wasn't what we wanted to hear. For a moment, we were confused. While grappling with this doctor's words that day, I decided to call Alora, a woman I knew from our parenting class at Baker Victory in 1998. She and her husband Dave adopted their daughter a few weeks after we adopted Marissa and we stayed in touch over the two years. She was a spiritual person whose opinion I valued.

When I explained what the pediatrician said, she cried into the phone, "You HAVE to go get her! Ignore that doctor! God put Madeline in your path for a reason. You are her parents."

That was precisely what I needed to hear. Terry and I both thought EXACTLY what Alora said, despite that medical professional's cautionary and uncaring words. I cried out of relief and excitement. Now it was perfectly clear to me; everything would be okay. And besides, we would, of course, handle any special needs Madeline had. I'm very thankful for Alora, who enabled us to listen to what our hearts and instincts were telling us.

We began the difficult game of waiting for the phone to ring with news of our travel date. We were anxious to go back to Russia and bring Madeline home, since we were confident that good food, lots of love and attention would make Madeline whole. She deserved a chance at a good life and we were eager for her to begin living it. The thought of our daughter being alone, on the other side of the world was nearly unbearable, making the wait seem much longer because of it.

One day, Marissa yelled, "I can't wait anymore for my new baby!" She loved her new sister and wasn't shy about showing it.

Our wait ended up being twenty-four days. As usual, we weren't given much notice. EAC called on Tuesday, February 20, to tell us we would be traveling Monday, February 26. We also received the wonderful news that we'd only be away for five days, returning back to Buffalo on Friday, the second of March.

We excitedly and hurriedly packed and completed the last minute paperwork for our trip. I made arrangements for Marissa to stay once again at my sister Peggy's house for three days and at home with my sister Joanne for the last two days. My sisters were making plans to assemble a big group to greet us at the airport Friday night with balloons, banners and well wishes.

It was a relief that such a short trip was planned.

When Marissa woke up the day we were leaving, I said to her, "Today, you are going to Aunt Peggy's house."

She responded, "Why I go to Aunt Peg's?"

"Because today we are going to get your new baby sister," I responded.

"Yay!" she yelled and proceeded to get ready to go.

The difficult waiting was finally behind us, or so we thought.

We didn't bring much luggage this time. We had a suitcase for Madeline's things and one for ours. We had no gifts this time around.

Our flight was uneventful and we arrived safely in Moscow on Tuesday morning, February 27. Irina picked us up at the airport and on the car ride to the hotel, she turned around from the front seat and delivered some bad news.

She told us that our court date was moved to Friday, the second of March, which was three days later than originally scheduled. That meant we needed to spend three full days hanging around Moscow with absolutely nothing to do before we traveled to Smolensk.

Terry and I were angry. They had known this information and yet, they had waited to tell us until we arrived at six in the morning in Moscow. Really? We could've stayed at home with Marissa, not inconveniencing Peggy and Joanne, and waited the extra three days in Orchard Park. It also meant that poor Madeline would spend three additional unnecessary days in her orphanage. Was this a case of the Russian government maximizing the monetary benefit of these adoptions? We would be spending our money in their capital city because our trip suddenly became three days longer. Our spirits were low and we were hungry, sad and tired. We had been awake for twenty-five hours at that point.

Irina and the driver took us to the Radisson Hotel, where we spent slow, leisurely days, once again acting like tourists. One day, it was very cold, zero degrees outside, and Irina asked if we were sure we wanted to go sightseeing. We were going stir crazy and decided to go outside with Irina as our tour guide. We shopped for souvenirs on Arbat Street, a pedestrian street in the historical center of Moscow. We had lunch at McDonald's and went to the GUM Department Store.

We stopped in a Russian post office, which was like something you would see in an old-fashioned wild west movie. I bought a postcard and wanted to mail it to Marissa back home. There was a barrel on the floor into which you were supposed to "mail" your letters. I asked Irina if the postcard would find its way to our house in Orchard Park. She shrugged in resignation and answered, "It might." It never did arrive.

We went to the movies at the American cinema in the hotel and watched a movie in English with Russian subtitles. I even ordered popcorn. We also toured Red Square again. This time, we didn't bring very warm clothes, thinking we would be inside most of the short trip. Well, we were obviously wrong. The trip was much longer than we planned.

One evening, Terry went out to dinner with Reggie and Sandra and I stayed at the hotel. I couldn't bear the thought of eating in a Russian restaurant just then. Terry reported back that the food was excellent and they had had a nice time.

We were not sleeping well at all and talked late into the night about Madeline. Terry started a countdown of how many days and hours she had left in her orphanage. And we thought the waiting at home for the travel date phone call was hard? That was nothing compared to this wait, the complete lack of control over our own destiny was infuriating.

Because our court date was set on Friday, March 2, that meant that we would be spending the entire weekend in Moscow with Madeline, waiting to go to the American Embassy the following Monday. We figured the Russians set that Friday court date to maximize the amount of time we were going to spend in their country, another cause for annoyance.

One new development that eased the pain was discovering we had access to email in the hotel business center. There was nothing like this in 1998 when we were in Russia with Marissa. This time, I was able to email my mother and Peggy to give them updates on our trip. Email was just gaining popularity. Not everyone had email addresses yet. We received emails back with news of home and Marissa. This new-found connectedness helped buoy our spirits.

Chapter THIRTEEN

Friday finally arrived and at five-thirty in the morning, we met Irina, the driver, Reggie and Sandra in the hotel lobby. It had snowed the night before and the temperature was frigid. We were going to drive with six adults in a crowded Mitsubishi SUV for five-and-a-half hours out to Smolensk. Once there, we were going to take care of all the legalities and government-required paperwork on that single day and drive back to Moscow by ten o'clock that night. We had needlessly waited around for three days, doing nothing just to have a jam-packed twenty-hour "marathon" day.

The bumpy ride out to Smolensk in the SUV was hard on us since we were tired from not having slept much the night before. We tried to rest on the way but it was difficult because we were dressed up in business attire for court and the SUV was very crowded. We stopped for fuel and Irina opened a basket and offered us open-faced sausage and salami sandwiches to eat by the side of the road. We each had a bottle of water. I wasn't able to eat much because that sausage didn't smell too appetizing to me.

Once we arrived in Smolensk, we went straight to court to adopt Madeline. The judge was a man this time, dressed in a pair of jeans and "mules" shoes, which were slip-on shoes with no backs. He completed his ensemble with a suit jacket and a tie. I thought it was such a bizarre outfit.

A social worker named Galina was in court, along with the Krasny Bor Baby House Medical Director, Svetlana. They both gave their opinions to the judge regarding our suitability as parents. Irina loosely translated a condensed version of their remarks for us. Terry answered questions about why we wanted to adopt, describing the type of parents we were. I sat quietly, listening to him. We were required to bring a photo of our four bedroom house and the prosecutor asked how many families lived in our home in Orchard Park. His puzzled face communicated his incredulity when we answered, "Just us."

When the proceeding was over and the judge was out of the courtroom deliberating, the prosecutor requested to speak privately with Terry. Immediately, Terry and I got a little nervous. Another meeting summons? What did this guy want? It turns out, he was very curious about the U.S. legal system and the type of law Terry practiced that afforded us the house in which we lived. They enjoyed a friendly exchange about the differences in the Russian and United States legal systems, the roles attorneys play in those systems and the compensation they received doing so. The man said that in Russia, the government can sue someone for getting injured, not the injured person, themselves. It was a confusing and complicated system.

The judge returned and officially announced that we were Madeline's parents. Everyone smiled and we hugged as I, of course, cried. The Russians seemed genuinely happy for us. The Baby House medical director told us Madeline was weak and had a cold. We were so anxious to get over there and pick her up.

We waited in the cold hallway while Reggie and Sandra had their day in court, which went just as smoothly as ours.

From there, we crowded into the SUV and headed to the vital statistics office so we could receive Madeline's adoption and birth certificates. The woman working there gave me a commemorative medal for Madeline because she was born in the city of Smolensk. It was a nice touch. That feeling quickly faded into something more sinister taking shape in my mind because when we received the birth certificate, it listed Terry and me as her birth parents. We didn't realize it or didn't think about it with Marissa, but in Russia, once a baby is adopted, officials alter the birth certificate and list the new adoptive parents as the birth parents. The documentation now appeared as if Terry and I were traveling through Russia nine months ago and happened to stop by in Smolensk and have a baby. We were taken aback with the birth certificate alteration, but we were powerless to do anything about it.

I have often thought about that as the years progressed. When they were young, on their respective birthdays, the girls and I would say a prayer together, thanking God for their birth mothers. We thanked them for giving the girls life and allowing Terry and me to teach them how to live that life. We always acknowledged the love and selflessness of their birthmothers and hoped they knew that the girls were alright. I felt sad knowing the birth mother's name had been removed from the original birth certificate, not even allowing her the proper acknowledgement on the document. Who knows, though, it is possible the Russian government just issued us that new birth certificate and kept the original one on file.

After the vital statistics office, we stopped at Immigration to get Madeline's Russian passport. It was funny because they spelled her name Medlin Greys not Madeline Grace.

Once we had Madeline's birth certificate, adoption certificate and passport in hand, we realized that we had been given the WRONG birthdate for her. She was born July 6, 2000. Not June 7, 2000. We were so elated and relieved. That meant that Madeline was one month younger than we originally thought, which made her not so small for her actual age. She was just shy of her eight month birthday, not ninth month. We were happy to hear this news and couldn't believe we had been operating with the wrong information for three months. I made a mental note to have my mom call the stationery store to change the adoption announcements I planned to mail the following week.

We left the city of Smolensk and drove to the orphanage to finally pick up our Madeline. As we turned onto the now-familiar road into the woods, my stomach was in my throat, my heart beating rapidly. We went inside and waited in the medical director's office. While waiting, we asked if we could see where Madeline slept so we could take a picture of her crib. EAC told us not all the orphanages allowed this. Fortunately, this one did.

Terry and I were led upstairs where we walked into a large room and there was Madeline, lying on a table while a woman changed her. Terry asked to pick her up. He kissed her, handed her to me and took our picture. Our hearts sang with love and happiness. I wept with the overwhelming relief we felt, once again having her in our arms. We were never letting her go. Miraculously, her eye no longer shook, her ear was no longer folded over. We wondered, did Madeline receive more attention and care in the past few weeks, now that she had a new family?

We realized we were in the room where Madeline spent her days. Bright, well-lit and warm, the room held several playpens and baby seats. I counted fifteen babies and a handful of ladies, sitting on the floor and in chairs, holding and playing with the kids.

Madeline's crib was in a small, dark room, adjacent to the one we were in. Fifteen or twenty cribs lined the room, with a few placed in the middle. Madeline's crib, the last one on the left side near the window, was labeled Number Two. Hung at the head of the crib, tied with a pink ribbon, was the crib medal I had left for her a month ago. I took a picture of the crib and was heartened, knowing the orphanage followed my wish of having the religious medal placed there, a small but significant gesture representing their compassion.

Back in the main room, I held Madeline and whispered in her ear "Let's go home Madeline. Say goodbye." We took her and never looked back.

We went back down to the medical director's office and got Madeline dressed in the clothes we brought with us. We were provided a written copy of her daily schedule. She woke up at six o'clock in the morning, was fed and washed up. During the day, she took three naps totaling six hours before being put to bed for the night at six o'clock in the evening. The schedule showed that Madeline spent only six hours each day out of her crib. We weren't sure whether to believe it. Chances are, this was "padded" to make it look like she didn't spend her entire day in her crib. She was fed mashed bananas, vegetables, meat, chicken, fish and eggs. No milk or formula. We were also told that in the eight months of her living there, no one from her birth family had ever come to visit her.

Outside in the cold, I snapped a few pictures of Terry holding Madeline before we got into the waiting SUV. The ride back to Moscow was incredible. Madeline was a bundle of pink. Dressed in a soft sleeper with a beret on her head, she was wearing a warm snow suit and was wrapped in a plush blanket. All soft pink. She looked adorable and I had visions of a quiet, calm, cozy ride with her being perfectly content to be cuddled and held the whole way to Moscow. We started out like that for a few minutes but then the party started. We quickly realized that our new baby was wiry and squirmed around constantly!

The SUV was overcrowded with six adults and two children. There were no seatbelts or car seats. Reggie was in the front with the driver and Sandra, Terry and I were in the back seat with Luba and Madeline on our laps. Irina rode in a small jump seat in a third row. We drove like this for five hours. Luba was adorable but very hungry. Sandra, a new mom, asked our advice on what we thought she could eat, since we had our own two-year-old at home. Luba liked Teddy Grahams and nearly ate the whole box.

Meanwhile, Madeline was ALL OVER THE PLACE. Laughing and smiling, playing and squirming, squealing and moving, grabbing things and putting them in her mouth. Sitting behind us, watching the whole show, Irina said she had NEVER seen a baby act like that coming out of an orphanage. She found Madeline's resiliency remarkable and asked us if she could take Madeline's picture. Irina laughed in disbelief as Madeline, Terry and I delighted in one another.

We juggled Madeline, fed her and juggled her some more. She was an engaging, joyful, charming and social little baby. By any standards, her personality was extraordinary. The car ride was a prelude for things to come; these traits would prove to be her most dominant and have stayed with her.

We arrived back in Moscow at ten o'clock that night, happy but road weary. We settled into the Radisson Hotel and after Terry fed Madeline a bottle, we laid her in a portable crib for the night. She fell asleep immediately and slept through the night, waking at eight o'clock in the morning. With her crib next to our bed, I observed her as she woke up. She was wide awake but completely silent, engaging in "finger play," a form of self-stimulation; behavior most commonly seen in kids on the autism spectrum. She was alert and content to amuse herself for as long as necessary. I took note of this behavior and quickly popped her out of her crib. From then on, whenever she started to finger play, we'd grab her hands, look into her eyes and tell her she didn't need to do that anymore.

Terry gave her a bath in the bathroom sink and she loved it. Smiling, laughing and squealing, she was trying to put the running water into her mouth. I was snapping pictures as Terry juggled slippery Madeline, laughing with her. We spent Saturday and Sunday in the hotel room, getting to know each other. Madeline's disposition remained upbeat, curious and happy. She moved around constantly, ate voraciously and slept soundly. Again, all things she would continue to do throughout her childhood.

The U.S. Embassy required that a Russian doctor examine Madeline before she was allowed entry into the U.S. The same doctor who would examine all our girls arrived at our hotel room. His English was good and he had a reassuring bedside manner. He stated that Madeline looked good and was only slightly delayed. He pointed out a few small holes at the base of her spine and he recommended we have them looked at by our pediatrician at home. We paid him seventy-five dollars in U.S. currency.

On Sunday, we heard that the Northeastern part of the U.S. was getting an epic snow and ice storm and flights out of Moscow were getting canceled. This added so much uncertainty; we couldn't bear to think we would be delayed any further than we already had been.

On Monday, Terry took Maddy to get her picture taken for the U.S. Embassy. I stayed at the hotel, having been told only one of us could go. At the U.S. Embassy, everything went fine and Madeline was cleared to go to the United States. Then it was time to pack to go home. We called Delta and they said it was likely that our flight on Tuesday morning would be canceled. All the flights from Moscow to NYC that day had been canceled and they needed to get those people back to New York as well.

Here's something unusual we learned during this trip: In Moscow, if you wanted to go somewhere, you simply went out into the street and flagged down any random car. If someone stopped, you jumped into their car and gave them cash. We were cautioned not to do this without a Russian coordinator with us. It was far too dangerous. We were told this WHILE we were in one of those such cars on an errand with our Russian coordinator. I guess you could call this Moscow's 2001 version of Uber.

Chapter FOURTEEN

We left the hotel early Tuesday morning and arrived at the packed and chaotic Moscow airport. Passengers whose flights were canceled the day before arrived that day, in hopes of getting on board. After waiting in a long line with all of our bags and a squirmy baby, we arrived at the Delta counter and the employee told us in a matter of fact tone that he did NOT have seats for us on the flight. I couldn't maintain my composure and began to raise my voice and get emotional, firmly stating that we needed to get on board that plane. I was running out of formula and diapers and couldn't last too much longer in that country. We had already been there for eight days.

The Delta agent and Terry both told me to calm down. "It will be better than you know," whispered the agent as he leaned over the counter, sensing my distress. What did he mean? He refused to elaborate but told us to go through to the gate and wait, which we did, along with a huge crowd of other parents, babies and toddlers.

While we waited at the gate, other people were getting their seat assignments handed to them. We got nothing. I was beside myself, thinking we were not getting on that plane. Other moms were giving me sympathetic glances.

Finally, as the plane began boarding, the Delta agent appeared and gave us our seat assignments: 1A and 1B. We didn't understand.

He smiled and said "It's first class."

At that time, a first class ticket from Moscow to New York was five thousand dollars per ticket, something we never even considered. This man arranged for us to travel in first class with no up-charge whatsoever. We were giddy with relief and excitement!

Terry and I thanked him profusely, grabbed those boarding passes and scurried onto the plane before anyone could stop us. It was wonderful. I can't describe the relief we felt. After we settled into our front row, first class seats, the flight attendants gave us a bowl of mixed nuts and a glass of wine as we waited for everyone else to get on board. People who originally felt sorry for us at the gate now passed us as they proceeded to their own seats back in coach. They looked at us with relief, but also with a hint of envy in their eyes.

Because we were seated in the first row, the flight attendant gave us a bassinet that could be attached to the front wall of the cabin. Madeline could lie in there and sleep during the flight. Foolishly forgetting her disposition for a moment, we thought we'd be relaxing for the long flight. We fed Madeline and placed her in the bassinet. She lay down, all nestled in for about thirty seconds and then popped up, smiling, trying to climb out, NEVER to return to that thing for the rest of the trip. The flight attendants were so smitten by her and her engaging personality that they took turns holding her, talking with her, walking around with her, laughing and cooing, giving us a break while we ate our delicious dinners.

First class meant spacious, cushioned seats that lay back flat, before personal pods became the norm. The food was served a la carte and we ate off china plates. A dessert cart was pushed around for us to make our own ice cream sundaes.

The seat next to us was reserved for the pilot to rest and eat during the eleven-hour flight. We struck up a long, friendly conversation with him as he ate dinner. He mentioned he always flew that same roundtrip New York-Moscow route and he greeted the passengers boarding and disembarking the plane. We explained that Madeline was our second baby and that this was our sixth flight with him. We enjoyed his company and after a while, he wished us a nice flight and went back to the cockpit.

We arrived in New York and while going through customs, we were told that a new immigration law had been put in place the week prior. The Child Immigration Act of 2000 stated that foreign-born children would automatically attain U.S. citizen status when they landed on U.S. soil, if they were adopted by one or two United States citizens. There would be no more citizenship ceremonies at the Buffalo Zoo, like we had with Marissa.

After we got our luggage, we saw Kelly, Tom and their boys. We didn't have to switch airports this time because JetBlue had begun service to Buffalo from JFK, but we were pressed for time and walked with them to the Buffalo terminal. My memories of the reunion are mostly of me apologizing for not being able to spend time with them and feeling bad they had to battle the snow-clogged streets of New York with two young toddlers, to come greet us. We barely had time to make our connecting flight to Buffalo. We loved seeing them, even for such a short visit, and we appreciated their support.

Terry, Madeline and I boarded our flight to Buffalo and again we were seated in the first row. Madeline sat on our laps and greeted each passenger as they boarded the flight, making eye contact, waving, smiling, and laughing at everyone. People giggled, smiled and waved back. Passengers seated around us watched Madeline holding court, as my heart swelled with love and pride for her. I considered telling them that we just adopted her a few days prior, but refrained from doing so. They'd figure it out soon enough when we landed in Buffalo to the waiting throng of family and friends.

The Bishop of the Diocese of Buffalo was on our plane that evening, but Madeline was causing more of a stir than he was. I didn't see him personally but if I had, I would've asked him for a blessing. He and I knew each other casually from the time I worked on the Catholic Charities corporate fundraising board a few years prior.

As we flew across New York State, our excitement was mounting. We were so eager to see Marissa and have her meet Madeline for the first time.

We were the first people off the plane in Buffalo. I was carrying Madeline and as we walked into the terminal, Marissa came running up to us, wearing an "I'm the Big Sister" t-shirt. Her cries of "Mommy and Daddy" were almost primal. We scooped her up and smothered her in hugs and kisses as we showed her the new baby. She kept touching our faces with her two little hands, as if she couldn't believe we were finally there, in the flesh.

Behind Marissa, we saw and heard the huge crowd waiting for us! Our siblings, parents, nieces, nephews and friends cheered and clapped and held banners, balloons and American flags. My father held a sign that read "FINALLY!!!! You were worth the wait!" The young kids of the family held a ten- foot banner that read "WELCOME HOME MADELINE!" The atmosphere was electric. We all hugged, cried and laughed. It was such a relief to be home at last.

Our group consumed the whole gate area. As the other passengers disembarked behind us, they realized the backstory of the charming baby from the front row. Many of them stopped to wish us well. Complete strangers were standing around watching us, clapping and crying. We never did see the Bishop get off the plane, nor did he stop to say hello.

We lingered at the gate for more than an hour, greeting everyone, telling them about Madeline and our Russian adventure. Dozens of people took turns holding the baby and she wasn't scared at all. She loved the attention and posed for countless pictures. She was reaching for the balloons, smiling at all her cousins as they met her and said hello for the first time. She looked darling, playing to the crowd in her little pink beret. To this day, Madeline gets energy from interacting with people just like she did that evening in the airport.

At last, it was time for Terry, Marissa, Madeline and me to go home. This time, we didn't have our extended family over to our house. It was just the four of us. We got the kids ready for bed and then Marissa helped Terry feed Madeline her bottle as she effortlessly slipped into her new role as big sister and Mommy's helper. It was a dream come true for all of us!

Chapter FIFTEEN

Life began with our two little girls. In the first few days, we discovered that Madeline was extremely ticklish. We put her in the highchair and gave her food to eat with her fingers. After dinner, when I washed off her little hands, she was squirming, squealing, laughing and pulling away her hands. I had no idea that palms of hands could be ticklish, but hers definitely were.

Cards, gifts and notes arrived daily in the mail or were dropped off by friends, family and well-wishers. It was so touching that people felt such happiness for us. Most remembered to include a little token for Marissa, which made her feel special. I spent my evenings writing over a hundred thank you notes. People's love and generosity was wonderful. Because of that outpouring of support, I have always made sure I promptly acknowledge a new baby born to family and friends.

We had a lot of visitors in the first few weeks. Madeline enjoyed seeing everyone and continued to be such a joyful baby. She was very underweight and had a cold, but otherwise, got a clean bill of health from the pediatrician. He wasn't alarmed, but to be safe, I did take her to Children's Hospital for an MRI of her spine. She had three sacral dimples at the small of her back, at her tailbone. One was quite deep. Thankfully, the MRI ruled out any abnormality of her spinal cord.

One day, when my mother was over, I decided to give Madeline a bath in our kitchen sink. My mother turned around and had her back to me. I realized she was upset by something so I asked her what was wrong. She answered, "I've never seen a skinny baby before and it's so sad." Despite her small size and low weight as a baby, Madeline would go on to grow to be five-feet, nine inches with a lean, muscular build.

Three weeks after coming home, we had Madeline baptized at Nativity of Our Lord in Orchard Park. Even though it was Lent, they granted special dispensation to quickly baptize her for us. After the morning baptism, we had a wonderful party at our house, which went until midnight that night! No one wanted to leave.

In April, I took the two girls to Florida with my niece Caitlin. Terry met us a few days later. My parents were there and soon, about twenty other extended family members joined us. Madeline loved the pool and the beach but particularly relished all the attention from the many people vacationing with us.

Because we were still getting to know Madeline, we didn't quite understand that she was the type of person who could operate on little sleep. A bunch of us went out to a bar and I left Caitlin at the motel to babysit. We had so much fun, staying out and drinking and doing karaoke, of all things, until two-thirty in the morning. Madeline woke up an hour and a half later, at four a.m. for the day! Poor Terry got up with her and let me sleep. That was the last time we stayed out that late.

During the initial months in the United States, the plentiful and nutritious food, abundant love and attention and near constant human touch yielded remarkable results. Madeline was blossoming before our very eyes and the resiliency of her human spirit was incredible to observe. Gone was the self-stimulating finger play. Gone was her silence upon awakening. All of her little problems that once worried us disappeared. She was learning, absorbing, and growing. She absolutely adored Marissa. An extremely active child, Madeline was daring, fearless, and fast. Despite the lack of muscle tone when we met her initially, she developed powerful upper body strength and learned to hang-jump out of her crib at ten months old. She climbed in drawers, in the tub, and in the toilet. She scampered up on the countertops and the table. She licked anything and everything she could get her hands on. We called 911 on a few occasions when we couldn't find her and also had to call the Erie County poison control hotline when she got into things she shouldn't have.

Madeline kept Marissa and me very busy, chasing after her during the day. When we'd catch her, she'd yelp and squeal with pure delight. On the weekends, she spent a lot of time up on Terry's shoulders, a place where we could keep track of her and where we knew she was safe. She took her first steps right on cue on her first birthday. She was the happiest baby! She played peek-a-boo with people in the grocery store, blew kisses to neighbors and giggled and smiled all day long. With her curly white hair piled in a little fountain atop her head and her cute upturned nose, people routinely said she looked like a little pixie and asked me if she ever cried. She rarely did. She was pure joy but was in CONSTANT motion, full of mischief and commotion and was very difficult to hold. She was so wiry due to her ticklishness and her desire to be free.

No longer was Madeline just surviving. Now she was thriving. So was Marissa, who learned to rollerblade on the carpeted basement floor at two years old and had our neighbor, Bubba take the training wheels off her bike when she was three years old. Determined and driven, she used her athleticism to propel herself forward to do whatever the "big kids" were doing. Marissa remained a serious but extremely loving and thoughtful toddler, always making sure that Madeline had what she needed or wanted.

Like we did with Marissa, we adopted Madeline in Surrogate's Court in Buffalo. Her birth certificate would now be on file in Albany, NY. This was convenient throughout the girls' childhood years when we needed birth certificates to sign up for school and other activities.

We submitted our required monthly post-placement reports to EAC and had the Baker Victory Services social worker visit us for Marissa's and now Madeline's regular reports. Although we complied with these paperwork requirements, it was difficult because life with Madeline was a whirlwind and we were busy, from the time her eyes popped open in the morning to the moment she began to thankfully suck her fingers at the end of the day. Marissa started a preschool program and had ice skating lessons, a little soccer league, and gymnastics, which also kept us busy.

Some days our house looked like a tornado hit it and I found solace in having our regular babysitter, Miss Donna, a grandmother-type help me one morning a week so I could take a break from chasing Madeline and accomplish the tasks necessary to run a household. I was also able to fulfill my duty as chair of the board of directors of Cradle Beach Camp. I no longer worked part time from home for Verizon. There just wasn't room in our schedule. I started a neighborhood play group, where other stay-at-home moms and I would get together with the kids once a week. I'm still friends with some of the ladies today.

My mother, mother-in-law, sisters and sisters-in-law all chipped in to help me and I was, and still am, so thankful for their support.

Periodically, Terry and I would bring the girls to the EAC seminars where I would speak about our experience to prospective adoptive parents. I remember always telling them that adopting children from Russia was a beautiful way to build a family, but most definitely not for the "faint of heart." In addition to the cost and administrative requirements involved, the emotional agility one needed was difficult to describe in meaningful terms. I ended up mentoring several local families through the process. Talking to the families gave us the courage and motivation to eventually add yet another new baby to our family. Looking back, I think it is a miracle that we added another baby to the mix after Madeline because she was such an active child!

An interesting side note here: Marissa and Madeline are twenty-five months apart in age, almost to the day. Their birth dates are June 4, 1998, and July 6, 2000, respectively. Coincidentally, our next baby would continue the pattern. Katherine Claire was born on August 6, 2002, exactly twenty-five months younger than Madeline, to the day.

Chapter SIXTEEN

In the fall of 2002, I called EAC and told them we wanted to adopt another baby. None of the previous paperwork was valid. We had to assemble the whole dossier and file the necessary paperwork all over again, as if we were first time adoptive parents. I found this frustrating. We'd just done this a mere eighteen months before. Nothing in our health or financial status had changed. But we had to start from scratch. This time, I didn't have time to keep fastidious records and felt like I was "winging" it through the process. I used the evenings to complete paperwork because during the daylight hours, I was swept up in the joyful chaos that was our family. Nevertheless, I completed the now-familiar tedious heap of paperwork by Christmas. I became friends with our FedEx guy, who one time said, "I can't believe you're doing this again!" Well, believe it or not, we requested TWO babies. I don't know, were we brave or just plain crazy? We were already thirty- eight years old and felt that time was running out to build the big family we wanted.

The first referral came in the winter of a darling boy about thirteen months old. The orphanage nicknamed him "The Mayor," due to his outgoing personality. The video we received showed him blond and blue-eyed, walking around, waving to the camera. Terry and I both were smitten. We could picture him fitting in with our family, but we were a little worried due to his age. That placed him only about a year younger than Madeline. Could we handle two so close in age?

I called EAC shortly after receiving the video and learned an important lesson: Don't ask a question if you're not ready to hear the answer. I asked why this delightful boy hadn't been adopted already. Thirteen months was older than most babies being adopted. I was told that because I asked, they were obligated to tell me. He was part of a sibling group and they'd been unable to place them together, so they were splitting them up. I told them that we could not be part of such a thing. I hung up and cried. I cried for this little boy and I cried for his siblings. I cried for us and the loss we already felt, having connected to him only through a short video. It was awful telling Terry that news.

Several months later at an EAC adoption seminar in a hotel meeting room, we were speaking to a group of prospective adoptive parents. There was a panel of families, all speaking about their experiences. Wouldn't you know it, that little boy walked by Terry and me. I thought I was seeing a ghost. Terry and I looked at each other with shock in our eyes, but we didn't say a word. That little boy ended up being adopted by a local family and they all seemed so happy. He was just as adorable in person as he'd been in the video. I have no idea if his new family knew his backstory and we didn't ask.

Terry and I have thought about that little boy periodically throughout the years and it still makes us sad. It prompted me to wonder why I never asked that question about Marissa or Madeline. I decided not to ask with the next referral.

We continued to wait and filled our days with love, laughter and family. If the baby was a girl, we decided we would name her either Katherine Noelle or Claire Elizabeth. We both loved the names.

Each call I placed into EAC was met with the same response: "Things are moving much slower now with Russian adoptions. You have to be patient and wait." The Russian government changed the adoption process in response to a few tragic adoption stories. They made a new law requiring the American adoption agencies be re-certified to conduct adoptions in Russia. This is what caused the delay.

On one of the calls, I discovered that Claire, who referred us to Marissa, had died. Saddened by this news, I decided to change our name choices and combine our two ideas. Terry liked it. If the baby was a girl, she would be Katherine Claire.

Chapter SEVENTEEN

Finally, five months after completing the paperwork, the phone rang on May 22, 2003. It was Sharon from EAC. They had a baby for us and it was a girl! Her name was Nastya, which is a nickname for Anastasia. Sharon said she was born back in July 2002 and had light hair and blue eyes. We were thrilled to learn that the baby lived in the Murom Infant Home, the same place as Marissa. This wasn't too unusual because EAC only was certified or licensed to operate in a few regions in Russia. Many Russian kids living in the WNY area were adopted from the same regions.

We were so happy that it would be an easy trip in Russia and one that was familiar. We wondered if we'd be staying with a host family again or if we'd see the same coordinators in Vladimir. We decided that when we did travel to the Murom Infant Home, we'd show them pictures of Marissa and ask if she had any birth siblings in the system. We were ready to hear whatever answer they provided. We also hoped we'd see Gara, Marissa's wonderful caregiver again. Like with Madeline, this adoption meant two trips to Russia.

Besides the baby's gender, all of the initial information we were provided turned out to be incorrect. Her medical report was typical but that also turned out to be wrong. When we eventually met her, we saw that Katherine Claire had brown hair, brown eyes and we learned she was born on August 6, 2002. This was great news, because she was actually a month younger than we originally thought.

The baby's photos were adorable and showed a healthy-looking, full-cheeked baby, just not one that was almost a year old. We watched the video and the baby looked beautiful, other than being delayed in her development. She was unable to sit up on her own like a child her age in the U.S. The girls were so excited that Madeline hugged the TV. Marissa set about making the baby an "I love you" card and we went to the store to pick out a special doll for us to take to Katherine.

The medical report indicated she was six pounds at birth and was carried to full term. It also said she had perinatal encephalopathy, which is acute or subacute brain injury due to asphyxia.She had motion disorder syndrome, a functional heart murmur, a cold, bronchitis, anemia, and hypotrophy, which is the enlargement of an organ, although it didn't indicate a specific organ. It also said she had rickets, a disease caused by a vitamin D deficiency. By now, we were so accustomed to these diagnoses and had seen similar ones on Marissa's and Madeline's reports, that we were prepared to ignore all of them.

We decided to accept the referral, but we sent the information and video to Dr. Chasnoff in Chicago for his opinion so we would know what we were dealing with.

Dr. Chasnoff gave us his opinion on the third of June. He said developmentally, Katherine was two or three months old but he couldn't tell her actual age by looking at her. She was not able to roll over or sit up on her own. He explained that the longer the babies were in the orphanage, the more delayed they were. His opinion was that she was "quite delayed." He said she had good weight gain until she was five months old and then she was "completely neglected." This was heartbreaking to hear, and later we learned that Katherine was with her birth mother until she was six months old. Then she was placed in the orphanage, for reasons still unknown to us today. I was happy she had the care and love of her birth mother for those first formative months, but was sad thinking of the trauma she endured being separated from her at six months old. That still hurts me when I think about it.

Dr. Chasnoff said, like Marissa and Madeline, Katherine had no signs whatsoever of fetal alcohol syndrome, which was extremely common with Russian orphans. We were fortunate this was the case. He said all the babies had rickets and that it self-corrected once they were home. He ended his remarks on a high note, saying Katherine looked better than most Russian orphans they saw at the Child Study Center.

After accepting Katherine's referral, Terry and I changed our minds and decided to only adopt one baby this time, abandoning the idea of adopting two babies simultaneously.

We heard from Diana at EAC. We would be traveling to meet Katherine on Saturday, June 28, which was only three and a half weeks away! It was so exciting and I kicked into action with all the arrangements. I had to juggle the girls' bedrooms to make room for a baby in the nursery, break a lease on our SUV and purchase a minivan so we could fit three car seats, and find babysitters for Marissa and Madeline while we were away. We began our packing, organizing and of course, began that "white-knuckle ride" of the last minute Russian visa paperwork. Interestingly, the fees for the Russian visas had doubled since the last time we applied in March 2001.

Diana told us we'd need to bring three thousand five hundred dollars in new U.S. currency, with a specific request that it be fifties and hundreds only. We also needed to get a ten thousand-dollar cashier's check payable to a woman named Vickie and mail it to EAC in Ohio three days before we left. These were new procedures. I can't remember bringing any gifts, but I wrote in my file that we had five hundred dollars to be used as gifts. On our second trip, we'd be bringing three thousand dollars in cash, again in new fifties and hundreds.

The week before we were scheduled to leave, our travel date got moved. We would be leaving on Tuesday, June 24, 2003, to go meet Katherine. This caused more stress with the last minute scramble for Terry to arrange his work schedule and for me to change the babysitting arrangements. Terry was in the midst of working on one of the biggest cases of his career as a personal injury attorney. A client suffered a life-altering, debilitating injury and he was scheduled for trial in July. His stress level was extremely high.

Chapter EIGHTEEN

Leaving Buffalo on Tuesday, June 24, was difficult. The weather was beautiful and my parents came over to get Marissa and Madeline. Madeline was going to Erie, Pennsylvania, to stay with our friends, Noelle and Lefty. Marissa was going out to my sister Peggy's cottage to stay with her family, the Hillerys. It was an exciting time of the year because school had just let out for the summer for Peggy's four kids and there was lots of fun to be had at the cottage. Madeline was so happy to jump into Gram's car and she excitedly exclaimed, "I'm going to Pencileeria!" Marissa, on the other hand, couldn't even say goodbye. She was frowning and had tears in her eyes, clearly distraught with the idea of us leaving. I knew she'd have a wonderful, fun-filled time at the cottage, but looking at her was so sad and distressing. We kissed them good bye and told them we'd see them this upcoming weekend. We had a quick, whirlwind trip in store for us and we were scheduled to be back home that Saturday, June 28,, only five days from then. Our second trip, scheduled for July 13 through July 23, would be much longer.

Our flight from JFK to Moscow was uneventful although we saw our pilot friend and said hello. He laughed that we were "at it again," as he said.

We landed in Moscow on Wednesday, June 25 where Michael, by now a familiar friend, promptly picked us up. As we drove to the Radisson Hotel, we took note of the remarkable changes in Moscow. It had been five years since our first trip. It seemed like THIS Moscow was a new city we hadn't yet experienced. The first big change was that there was no snow! This was our first summer trip, and it was hot outside. There were no fur coats. The cars were still dirty, all crammed on the eleven lane street, but now many were imported vehicles. Everything seemed so westernized.

Luxury goods stores, like Gucci and Prada had popped up. There were car dealerships, offering high end SUVs. Billboards, advertising Hollywood movies and American brands were on the side of the street. Satellite dishes adorned every apartment balcony and there were kids on skateboards and rollerblades. There were even rowers on the Moscow River. There were numerous signs written in English, making the city seem less foreign and more cosmopolitan. There was a beehive of construction going on, cranes dotting the skyline. It was all very different than in 1998. Having been there three times before, we definitely felt more at ease this time. Only five years had elapsed, but the world seemed a whole lot smaller than it had in 1998.

Again, we stayed in the Radisson Hotel and due to jet lag, slept most of the day. We grabbed dinner in the hotel lobby bar and were approached by an American couple. The man said to Terry "I can tell you're American because you're the only person in Moscow wearing shorts." We laughed and introduced ourselves. This was Juan and Vickie[11] from Florida, two wonderful people who were adopting twin girls from Katherine's orphanage. We would be traveling with them to the Vladimir Region the next day at six o'clock in the morning.

That night, we couldn't sleep that well. The Russian "white nights" took us completely by surprise. No one mentioned we would encounter this. Because of Moscow's latitudinal position and because it was only four days from the summer solstice, it started to get light outside at two forty-five in the morning. The sun rose for the day at three-thirty a.m. I woke up at three o'clock in the morning, thinking it was the afternoon. We were so confused and thought we missed our trip out to the region. I guess you could say we still weren't exactly savvy world travelers! More like country bumpkins, really.

I felt little or no anxiety on the trip. I was familiar with the whole drill and had grown accustomed to the ways Russians did business. I didn't feel anxious about our safety because we knew the Radisson Hotel and the neighborhood. It was such a pleasant change to experience the trip without being crippled with anxiety.

We traveled out of Moscow to Vladimir by car with a driver and Vickie and Juan. This time, we saw a suburb with nice houses, which had been developed since the last time we were on that road. It was a small suburb, only a few streets, but it was similar to what you would see in America.

It was a two-and-a-half hour, one hundred ten-mile ride to Vladimir and we spent the drive getting to know Vickie and Juan. We learned that they had two biological boys at home and that Juan was an entertainer. We thought he meant he played guitar and sang at the local bars and restaurants. Boy, were we wrong!

On the ride, it was mile after mile of dense, green forest with periodic small villages outside our van window. Terry and I had traveled this same road back in 1998, on our way to meet Marissa. Once again, just like in 1998, out in the middle of nowhere, people were selling the oddest things by the side of the road. Like before, they were selling stuffed animals, but now they were hawking swim floats, inflatable pools, rafts, chandeliers, vases, vegetables and beach towels. Who was going to buy such random things and where did these people even get these items to sell? We were in the middle of a desolate forest. Seeing this again was comical on one level, confusing on another and pathetic on yet another.

We went directly to the Murom Infant Home, which looked exactly the same on the outside as it did in 1998. Because it was summer, there were flowers planted in old tires on the front lawn. Although familiar, it was strange to be back there.

Inside, it smelled terribly of paint fumes and the halls were filled with junk because they were remodeling. We were not allowed to tour around this time at all.

As we waited to meet Katherine, my heart was beating very rapidly in my chest. They put us in a small office, with a desk, chair and yet again, a glass case that contained old fashioned, untouched and unused toys. A mangy black cat wandered by. A woman I had never seen before brought Katherine into the room. I felt overcome with emotion and had to sit down. Despite the warm weather, Katherine was dressed in a red corduroy one-piece outfit with pink socks and a white bonnet. She was adorable! She had brown eyes and a great big smile that revealed a darling dimple on her cheek.

When she was handed to us, she seemed a little scared and she frowned a few times but as time went on, she started smiling more and making noises and playing with the doll we brought. She liked to pull my hair and laughed out loud when she did it. We blessed her with Holy Water we brought with us and Terry and I took turns holding her, posing for pictures. Terry showed her the card

Marissa made for her. The orphanage, like all places in Russia, didn't have screens on their windows. Consequently, she had a lot of mosquito bites on her face and head. Katherine fell asleep in Terry's arms as the woman from the orphanage was telling us about her medical background.

We were able to spend three hours with Katherine in the large room where five years ago, we had first met Marissa. We fed her a bottle, laughed and played with her. Katherine was adorable, and we noticed she had a remarkable physical feature: she had very delicate hands with extremely long, graceful fingers. They were so unusual and very striking. She also had long, slender feet. It sounds funny to say, but her hands and feet were beautiful sights to behold.

We got the chance to meet Vickie and Juan's identical twin girls. We were all so happy at that moment; it was dreadful to think we'd be leaving the babies soon.

While we were there, we saw the Little Tykes Cozy Coupe car we brought back in 1998. The orphanage director claimed she remembered Marissa, and we showed her pictures of Marissa at five years old. She was delighted and kept the pictures. We asked if Marissa had any younger birth siblings in the Baby House and she left to check her records. She reappeared a while later and told us no, she didn't. If there were younger siblings, Terry and I were prepared to start the adoption process for them. We felt a mix of relief and sadness upon hearing the news.

I experienced a lot of emotions being with Katherine, love and longing being the two most prominent. I loved her with my whole heart and felt such longing to be home with her. With anxiety diminished on this fourth trip to Russia, I discovered I could more fully experience other emotions on a deeper level. I felt a longing for Katherine to be at home with her sisters, and I longed to be home with them too. It was so unsettling, having kids on two different continents. I wanted so badly to take her home with us that day. It was so unfair that she had to stay there after we left. I cried and held her and hugged her. She was ours. We were told it was time to leave and we said our goodbyes. It was awful.

We drove an hour to Vladimir and were pleasantly surprised that we would not be staying with a host family this time. We stayed in a newly-built, wooden hotel that was styled after the small motels in the Alps in Europe. It had a series of little separate German or Swiss looking wooden cottages. Goats were running around outside. The cottages were new and therefore immaculate, cozy, yet spacious.

We went to dinner in a separate building with Vickie and Juan. It was such an experience. My journal offers this: "The food you order here is never what you think it's going to be." I don't know what that meant. After dinner, there were dancers who came out to entertain us. We were the only customers in the entire place. It was a modest, family-style, casual restaurant and yet the dancers were dancing under a swirling disco ball, wearing elaborate Las Vegas showgirl-like costumes. It was so unexpected and incongruent with the surroundings. The four of us kept trying to stifle our laughter. We enjoyed the evening and were happy to talk about our families and the little babies we left behind only a few hours ago.

Once back at the cottage, we settled in for the night. Reality hit and Terry and I were miserable. He became extremely quiet. We didn't talk, we couldn't sleep and I kept crying, thinking of Katherine. It was horrible, knowing she was in that orphanage.

The next morning arrived and we drove back to Moscow. Due to traffic, the trip took four hours. We visited with Vickie and Juan on the ride and enjoyed becoming thier friends. Juan told us he was the star of a telenovela seen in Mexico and they had to explain to us that a telenovela is similar to our American soap operas. He told us he had a recurring role in a popular American TV series and hosted a regular segment on an entertainment show. Terry began what would become a standing joke.

"You're not famous Juan. We don't even know what a telenovela is!" Terry announced and we all laughed when we explained that the day before, we thought he was a corner bar singer.

"No no, people REALLY do know who I am," Juan explained.

"Yea, okay, right," Terry answered.

The exchange offered much-needed light heartedness!

Other than our banter, the ride was awful. Four hours of a bumpy ride, exhaust fumes, hunger and the driver's cigarette smoke made us all nauseous.

When we got back to Moscow, the four of us walked to McDonald's for a bite to eat. That meant crossing the eleven-lane road. We walked past homeless people on the street and some kids begging for food and money. The sight of that left an indelible mark on my memory.

We continued walking and--lo and behold--there was Juan on a billboard.

"See, Terry?! I REALLY am famous," Juan joked. We all laughed that he had to keep explaining to us, as we continued to feign disbelief. Really, we had never heard of him and never thought about the entertainment industry that stretched beyond Hollywood. Once again, we were reminded of our myopic view of the world.

When we arrived at McDonald's, a wedding reception was taking place there, complete with the bride in her elaborate white dress and the groom in a black suit. A maître d' sat us at our table. We laughed and spoke about it the entire time we were eating. Two unusual dinner experiences in a row.

Once back at the hotel, we emailed and called home. It was very sad to hear little Madeline's voice over the phone at Noelle and Lefty's house. It was just as bad to hear Marissa at Hillery's. I explained to each of them about their new baby sister and that we'd be leaving Moscow in the morning. I got my familiar anxiety-induced stomach ache after the phone calls and yearned to be home so we could hurry up and come back to pick up Katherine. Our hearts were heavy as we flew home but the flight went smoothly and nothing memorable happened.

When we arrived back home, we drove straight out to the cottage. Joanne picked up Madeline from Noelle and already had her in bed at the cottage for the night. Marissa was still down the street, at the Hillery's cottage. I came around the back of their cottage and when Marissa saw me, she jumped into my arms and just sobbed.

She clung to me and then whispered in my ear, "What does Katherine look like?"

After we put Marissa to bed, we sat on our front porch with Noelle, Lefty, Peggy and Joanne as we told them all about our quick trip. We enjoyed a few drinks and we gave them gifts we purchased in Moscow. They filled us in on the details of caring for our girls that week. Marissa had a wonderful time, spending carefree days with her cousins on the beach. Madeline loved being at Noelle and Lefty's and especially enjoyed spending time on Lefty's lap in their family room. They didn't say it, but we knew they all must have thought, "We have to do this all over again in two weeks!"

We so appreciated all their love, support and help. Without them and our entire extended families, we couldn't have done what we did. Like the saying goes, "it takes a village." It was so good to be home.

In the morning, Madeline was so happy and surprised to see us! All she was interested in doing was telling Terry and me about Noelle and Lefty's cat, Sylvester. She loved that cat and I imagined she must have terrorized the poor thing all week.

We enjoyed our first week home at the cottage and celebrated the Fourth of July with our annual neighborhood bike parade and evening fire on the beach. The weather was beautiful, a welcome break from the unusually soggy spring we had that year. We celebrated Maddy's third birthday on Sunday, July 6, with family at the cottage. For her gift, we invested in an elaborate playset for the backyard at our house in Orchard Park, hoping it would minimize the near constant climbing she was doing inside the house on the tables, cupboards and stairs. We purchased a truckload of rubber mulch to place under the playset to keep the kids safe, knowing Madeline would take daring chances on the playset. She loved the set and the indoor climbing stopped immediately. But, sure enough, my neighbor Kerri called me one day to tell me Madeline was walking across the top of the monkey bars. I responded, half-jokingly, "Don't look out your window!"

Fortunately, time passed quickly and soon it was time to begin preparing for our second trip to Russia.

Chapter NINETEEN

We were scheduled to leave Buffalo on Sunday, July 13, and return home ten days later on Wednesday, July 23. It was a long trip this time.

In addition to our own clothes, we packed clothes and supplies for Katherine and the three thousand dollars in U.S. currency, again in new fifties and hundreds only.

Terry was buried in his case at work and was preparing for the trial later that month, which had been scheduled well over a year in advance. It was all-consuming for him and we had to make an important and difficult decision.

For his client's sake and for his own commitment to his profession, Terry needed to come home early from Russia, alone on Saturday, July 19. Our wedding anniversary was the next day, July 20, and for the first time, I'd be spending that without him. I would be there alone with Katherine in Moscow for four days.

Besides the panic and dread this evoked within me, it created a need for additional paperwork since Terry would not be in Russia for the Russian Consulate paperwork. He signed over his power of attorney to me and there were affidavits and other forms to be completed before we traveled. EAC wasn't thrilled with the idea, but we stood firm that this was unavoidable, so they guided us through the process. I'm not sure they had done this before.

I couldn't even fathom the idea of a ten-hour flight alone with the baby. But there was no way around this; I began preparing myself to do what I had to do.

The night before we left for Russia, Terry and I put Marissa to bed. She cried and gave me ten kisses, one for each day I'd be away. Then she gave me some extra ones for Katherine. I cried silently as I rubbed Marissa's back and I left the room. Then she said to Terry, "I don't want anything to happen to my mom." Her little five-year old mind wouldn't allow her to relax and enjoy the carefree oblivion most children possess.

Madeline, too young to understand, remained blissfully unaware; she just went to sleep, like she always did.

On the morning of our departure Joanne moved into the cottage to watch the girls while my mother drove us to the airport. Marissa woke up to see us off. I had a sizable lump in my throat, unable to properly say goodbye. I just said, "I love you," kissed her and got in the car.

Our flight to Moscow was good and we both slept for a few hours. Over the Atlantic, I was thinking that we had children on both sides of that ocean, all of them without Terry and me at that moment.

When we arrived in Moscow, it was much warmer than we expected. They have a continental climate, bringing warm humid air to the area in the summer. That week, they were having a heat wave. It was hot: eighty-five degrees.

Terry and I checked into the now-familiar Radisson and rested. We enjoyed dinner on a boat in the Moscow River, followed by a relaxing swim in the hotel pool. We enjoyed each other's company, talking and laughing and then had a great night's sleep and felt "normal" in the morning.

Later that day, we met Vickie and Juan in the lobby for the drive out to Vladimir. Heavy traffic once again turned our two-and-a-half hour ride into four hours. Four hours of sweltering heat, exhaust fumes and cigarette smoke. It was nauseating. So much for feeling "normal."

We were told that the nice German-style cottage hotel in Vladimir was booked, so we had to stay in an old Soviet style high rise hotel, which cost us thirty U.S. dollars per night.

We had dinner with Vickie and Juan. He brought Terry a music CD of a concert he performed in Mexico City. Again, we joked that he was still trying to get Terry to admit he was "famous." We also discovered that during our two weeks home in the United States, Vickie went to Tampa and donated her bone marrow for someone in a European country, whom she'd never met before. She was a remarkable person and my relaxed and fun days at the cottage seemed slightly frivolous to me at the time.

After dinner, we walked around Vladimir and had a "Seinfeld-like" conversation about how in Russia, you order water with or without gas. Water is never offered for free in Russia and at every meal, we always ended up with carbonated water by mistake.

Terry joked to Juan, "You're so famous, go into that store and buy us some water without gas."

We all felt safe, relaxed and excited to get the babies.

The next day, July 16, was Katherine's adoption day. We were scheduled to go to court in the city of Vladimir. We hoped we had time to drive the two hours out to Murom to pick up the girls after we were finished.

The weather was so hot and humid and there wasn't a cloud in the blue sky, but we were dressed in business attire for court, clothes that were definitely not suitable for the sultry weather.

The court proceeding went very well. The judge was extremely stern until the end, when he wished our family much success and love. Of course, this made me cry.

After court, we had six stops to make at various official places like the adoption center and vital statistics. We were uncomfortable in our clothes so Terry asked Anya, our coordinator, if we could stop back at the hotel to change our clothes before driving to Murom.

She answered, "No, that's not a good enough reason."

The four of us laughed and Terry ended up taking his jacket, shirt and tie off and spent the rest of the day in an undershirt. Juan wisely had shorts, sneakers and a t-shirt with him. Terry was very envious. We were starving and began eating the paltry snacks we had brought with us in the car. Juan ate Dinty Moore stew from a can, using the handle of Vickie's comb as a fork. Again, we all laughed and commented on what a crazy situation we found ourselves in.

It was four-thirty in the afternoon by the time the official business was taken care of and we were going to pick up the babies. It took an hour-and-a-half to get there. Terry slept on the way while I watched the countryside go by. The forest was lush green and people were out swimming in rivers, lying in the grass and lazily enjoying the warm sun. Other people were by the side of the road, selling blackberries, blueberries and strawberries that grew wild in the forest. Anya told the driver to stop and she bought some of the wild strawberries and shared them with me. They were tiny, deep red, with a wonderful aroma-- the sweetest berries I ever tasted. When we finally pulled up to the orphanage, Terry awoke and we ran inside with such a sense of urgency. They brought Katherine right to us and she was still dressed in that red corduroy one-piece outfit she had been wearing two weeks prior.

She wasn't shy or afraid at all. We quickly changed her into an outfit from home and had her ready to go. She was adorable and so calm and serene.

When we asked to see her crib, we were led to a room with several small cribs and told Katherine's crib was up against the open screenless windows. That explained all the bug bites on her face.

The orphanage director was explaining her diet and her schedule. Again, it was pureed fish, chicken and vegetables. They said she slept twelve hours per night and took three naps during the day, each of which was two hours long. That put her in that crib for eighteen hours per day and she was nearing twelve months old. That was way too long for her to be in a small crib on her back. We didn't know whether to believe this information or not, but that's what they told us.

The workers came to say goodbye and Katherine had a big smile for all of them. When a black and white cat walked into the room, Katherine yelped out loud. She was so excited! This was the first clue we had to Katherine's lifelong love and passion for all things furry and four-legged!

On the ride back to Vladimir, Katherine was like an angel. Like with Marissa and Madeline, Terry wanted to be the one to hold her most of the way. She slept a little and other than that, she sat quietly and looked around. This was a glimpse we had into Katherine's disposition. She would, thankfully for us, turn out to be the most calm and well-behaved baby and toddler we could ever imagine having. Living with our beloved but crazy Madeline, this was a welcomed relief, knowing I wouldn't have to be chasing two kids!

When we got back to our Soviet-style hotel in Vladimir at nine o'clock in the evening, we walked to a store with Katherine. It stayed light outside until eleven-thirty at night. Katherine drank a bottle and slept well. In the morning, like our other girls, she too woke up and just quietly waited for me to get her out of her crib. She smiled whenever we looked at her, which was nearly constant, but other than that, she sat calmly and quietly, watching everything around her.

The ride back to Moscow went well. It felt so natural and easy to have Katherine with us, as if we had had her since birth. The long car ride helped us bond.

After the long, crowded and noisy ride back to Moscow, we settled into the Radisson and made phone calls home. The girls were having a great time at the cottage and Joanne organized all kinds of fun activities like "Backwards Day," "Pie Day," and "Field Trip Day." She kept a journal of their activities for us to read when we got home.

We gave Katherine a bath in the Radisson hotel and she LOVED it! She smiled, laughed and clapped the water. We fed her and put her to sleep for the night. She was like an angel and a dream, all in one.

That night was the first of two that Terry spent on the phone with his client, other lawyers, administrative assistants, paralegals and court administrators. All. Night. Long. It was regular business hours in the U.S. and he was in full work mode. He had decided not to tell anyone he was out of town, so as far as they knew, Terry was calling from his office in downtown Buffalo. The phone connection was crystal clear and I could hear Terry and the person on the other line. Katherine was never disturbed, thankfully.

Eventually, Terry decided to tell one person we were in Russia, who loudly responded, "I'M TALKING TO MOSCOW, RUSSIA?! ARE YOU KIDDING ME?!" It was funny.

Our hotel bill showed a total of eighteen calls made those two nights, each one lasting at least a half an hour. The bill was enormous. Terry was scheduled to fly back to the U.S. on Saturday for his trial on Monday. I needed to stay in Russia to go to the Russian Consulate four days after that.

Friday morning, the Russian doctor came to our hotel room to examine Katherine. It was the same doctor we had for Marissa and Madeline. We paid him ninety-five dollars in cash. His job was to examine the babies and give the parents the document they needed to present to the U.S. Embassy. He gave Katherine a clean bill of health and estimated her weight at twenty pounds.

He said, "She has remarkably long fingers and feet, doesn't she?" We laughed and said that yes, we noticed.

That day, we went to the American Embassy, which was filled with American families and their adopted children. It was a great experience, seeing them all. The process went very smoothly and Katherine was all set to come to America.

Since I would be in Moscow for a while with Katherine, we went to a grocery store for supplies like formula and diapers. It was so expensive there. We enjoyed Vickie and Juan's company as we placed all three babies on the floor in a little lobby area on our hotel floor. We enjoyed getting to know their adorable babies.

Katherine cried a lot that night and I was worried the formula wasn't agreeing with her. She was eleven-and-a-half months old by then and it was such a long time to be without us. We had a lot of catching up to do. At first, she was content by herself to play with her toys but after a mere two days of being with us, she grew accustomed to us holding her, playing with her and kissing her. We were spending those few days, forging a bond that was far too long in coming. She smiled every time one of us looked at her and she cried when one of us left the room! She'd stop and smile as soon as she saw us again. That was another sneak peek into her personality. She's quick to love and connect. She's also quick to forgive, a wonderful trait to have.

Terry was scheduled to leave the next day, Saturday morning. I had four days ahead of me, alone in Moscow with Katherine, waiting for the Russian Consulate appointment. Then I had the journey home with her, without him. I was afraid to be in Russia without Terry and afraid that if Katherine or I got sick, there was no one to help me. I was worried about hauling the luggage and the baby through the airport. I brought a baby carrier with me, but Katherine was too big and didn't fit in it. She also didn't fit into many of the clothes we brought for her. She was bigger than we expected. I did have Juan and Vickie next door, but they had their hands full with twins and that didn't ease my anxiety and sadness.

Katherine and I walked Terry to the front door in the lobby the next morning when he left for the airport. He claims he doesn't remember, but we both had tears in our eyes as we hugged and kissed our goodbyes. It was the strangest feeling, watching him get in the car with the driver. I felt so alone and so far from home. I was struggling to keep the panic from rising up in my throat. Katherine quickly snapped me out of my panic and melancholy by scratching my neck and chest with her fingernails. Nutrition from the food we had brought was causing her nails to begin growing like weeds. I needed to promptly find a store that sold little baby nail clippers.

The weather, like every other day on that trip, was gorgeous, sunny and hot without a cloud in the sky. Two Russian EAC employees, Alex and Anatoly took me, Katherine, Vickie, Juan and their twins on a tour of Moscow in a van. They took us to the Cathedral of Christ the Savior, a huge gorgeous cathedral with iconic golden onion domes. There was a lookout spot there with a panoramic view of the city of Moscow. It was beautiful and there were several brides and bridal parties there taking photos. Their cars were brightly decorated.

We went to Red Square, which was closed due to a terrorist threat. St. Basil's, the most famous of Russian churches, was covered because they were renovating it for the first time in five hundred years.

We ate at McDonald's, which looked exactly like our American McDonald's. The food was much saltier. Then we went to Arbat Street, a pedestrian street, which was so lively and festive in the summer. This was totally different from when we visited it in the winters of 1998 and 2001. I saw a young Russian girl, her hair pulled back with a gigantic bow, beautifully playing the violin, while her violin case lay open on the ground, a receptacle for her tips. I wondered how often she was there and what she did with the money she earned. There were vendors, street performers, markets, shops and food stalls. The enjoyable experiences made the day pass by quickly. For a few moments, I was able to forget my situation and feel like a regular tourist.

On Arbat Street, a Spanish-speaking woman practically swooned as she approached Juan and asked to have her picture taken with him. After she left, he and Vickie told me that some Spanish-speaking girls called their hotel room the night before because they couldn't believe he was there. We all agreed that it was a shame Terry wasn't there to witness all this.

Katherine was wonderful during the whole tour. She was very content and didn't make a sound. She just observed and smiled all day long.

That evening at nine o'clock, Katherine was asleep and I was in the room alone with her. It was still broad daylight outside. I calculated that Terry was two-and-a-half hours away from landing in New York City. I called the cottage and Joanne told me she and the girls were going down to Grandma Dot and Papa Jim's cottage to visit with the Atlanta cousins, who were in town for their annual vacation. I felt so lonely and anxious. It wasn't a good moment for me.

The next day, Sunday, July 20, was our twelfth wedding anniversary. At six o'clock that morning, I called home. It was ten o'clock in the evening Saturday night at the cottage. I spoke to Terry and was so relieved he was home safely.

I had purchased three Russian bells and sent Terry home with two of them. I asked him to have Marissa and Madeline ring their bells at bedtime. Katherine and I would ring our bell at the same time and we would all know that we were thinking of each other at that exact moment, physically apart, but together in spirit. He said Marissa and Madeline loved this idea and were ringing their bells like crazy. I also told the girls to look up at the moon in the evening and know that I, too, was looking at the same moon. It made the world seem just a little bit smaller for us.

Vickie and Juan treated me to lunch at the hotel in honor of my wedding anniversary that day. We all took a nice walk along the Moscow River. Katherine was wonderful. She was a calm baby, who smiled a lot. She began cutting a few teeth while we were in Moscow. She also started sitting up and learning to crawl. Her progress was amazing. Like the other girls, it was like watching a flower opening up in a time-lapsed video.

On Monday, Katherine started coming down with a cold. She had a hard time settling down for naps and cried a lot. I was worried about an ear infection. That day, our only activity was walking to the store. I bought a few souvenirs. I felt we had enough Russian souvenirs by then, but we had nothing else to do. There was a large crowd of EAC families who arrived in Moscow that day. We spent time down at the EAC office, chatting with them. One woman named Michelle from Columbus, Ohio, cried every time she mentioned her six- and three- year- old girls, left at home. I knew so well how she felt and could empathize with her. I listened as she cried, but had no advice to give her, because it never got easier.

Waiting those days to go home was difficult for me. They were so long and I yearned to be back in the United States with Katherine. One evening, I thought about how it must've felt for all three of my girls to wait in their orphanages, day after day, month after month. I thought of Marissa and Madeline waiting for me to get home. I told myself to stop feeling sorry and just embrace reality.

Katherine was up crying two times during the night. I had infant Tylenol with me and gave her a dose.

Our last full day in Moscow finally arrived. We got the paperwork from the Russian Consulate and we were scheduled to leave at ten-thirty in the morning the next day, Wednesday, July 23. If all went smoothly and as planned, I would be in the Buffalo airport tomorrow evening!

That last day turned out to be a great one. Katherine woke up and seemed fine. Vickie, Juan and I took the babies out for a walk and we were joined by a couple from Corpus Christi, Texas. They had a daughter named Hannah. We walked back to Arbat Street and went to lunch.

Hannah was a handful—full of energy and mischief. Her mom looked at Katherine and jokingly asked, "How did you get a calm baby?"

I laughed and told her, "Oh, I have a "Hannah" at home. Her name is Madeline. God graced me with a calm baby this time." I told her how much fun Madeline brought to our days and that I was sure Hannah would, too.

The next day, Katherine and I got up early to go to the airport. She wasn't feeling well and had a fever. I said goodbye to Vickie and Juan and wished them a safe flight home. They told me the Miami airport had a private room set aside for their family to greet them when they arrived home. Their adoption story made it onto the cover of a Spanish-language magazine.

Chapter TWENTY

My flight home from Russia alone with Katherine was unbelievable. It was a freak show. That's the only way I can describe it. The plane was huge with a double aisle, five seats in the middle and two seats on either side. It was a "baby flight," absolutely packed and incredibly loud and chaotic. The whole flight was during the daylight hours. It was loud with babies and kids and there was a lot of commotion with kids not being able to sit still. I was seated in the way back, in an aisle seat in the middle section of the plane. I only had one seat and Katherine was on my lap for the ten-and-a-half hour flight. It wouldn't be until early the next morning at our pediatrician's office that I found out that poor Katherine had a double ear infection. Can you imagine what flying must have felt like? She was running a fever and she cried most of the way home. I did, too.

I was seated next to a Sri Lankan named Eddie, an older gentleman who lived in Alaska. He was going home. Against his grown children's advice, he had flown to Russia to meet Marsha, his would-be mail-order bride. He had been communicating with Marsha and her mother for months, even sending her money, much to his children's dismay. When he arrived in Russia with a diamond engagement ring for Marsha, he discovered that she had no interest in marrying him; she only wanted him for his money. Poor Eddie was heartbroken and he talked and talked to me.

"Ja-nin, I am closing doors in my mind as we fly across the Atlantic," he said. "Why was Marsha so dishonest?" he asked over and over again. "She was an alcoholic, Ja-nin" he lamented. He told me all the minute, sad details of his pathetic failed quest for a bride, as poor Katherine cried and was slumped on my chest, burning up with a fever. The infant Tylenol wasn't doing too much to help her.

"Yeah, Eddie, that's sad. Listen, I'm sorry, but could you hold the baby while I go to the bathroom?" I asked after I listened to him for over an hour. When I returned, I told him we just adopted Katherine and he couldn't believe it. He claimed he never heard of a single person ever adopting a baby from overseas.

"Ja-nin. I cannot wrap my mind around what you are telling me," he said.

I thought, *Really Eddie? You know about Russian mail-order brides but not about Russian adoptions?* Poor Eddie. He was so distraught.

A few hours into the flight, the pilot, our friend, came back and happened to walk past my aisle seat.

I got his attention and when he saw me, he asked, "What are you doing way back here and why are you alone?" I attempted a feeble laugh and explained Terry had to go home early because of the trial. He said he was sorry that he just saw me and couldn't arrange for a first class seat. The plane was booked solid. He had me stand up as he pointed out the window. We were passing Iceland and he wanted me to see the icebergs in the sea.

We managed to get through the flight. Thankfully, Eddie dozed off. When we finally landed in New York, Katherine and I must have been a sight to behold, her limp and feverish and me just worn down. I waited for the huge plane to empty out. I gathered Katherine and our belongings and made my way to the front. The pilot was waiting for me.

"Come with me," he said. "I'll take you through a special line at customs for airline employees so you don't have to wait in the long line."

We sailed through customs and he told the agent, "Don't worry! She's with me!" The agent barely glanced at our documents.

I was so grateful I didn't have to wait in the long customs line and I will always be appreciative of his kindness.

He wished us well and said, "Maybe I'll see you guys again!" Of course, we never did.

As soon as I got my luggage, Kelly met me and Katherine. I was so road weary. So was Katherine. Kelly, alone this time, took the shuttle over to the Jet

Blue terminal at JFK with us. I changed Katherine into a fresh outfit and I visited with Kelly, telling her about the trip. I was so relieved to be home in the United States and I loved spending some time with Kelly. We weren't rushed like we were when we saw her with Madeline.

I've known Kelly since the third grade, love her and am honored to count her among my closest friends. It was so special and meaningful to have her there, celebrating our family all three times we adopted.

I boarded the flight to Buffalo and by then, Katherine was really struggling. She didn't look well. Pale and feverish, her eyes were red rimmed and swollen from all the crying. With no smiles to give, she was not her usual self. She was lethargic and miserable. She just clung to me and I to her.

We both fell asleep on the flight and I tried to gather myself when we landed in Buffalo. I knew there would be a huge contingency of friends and family at the airport waiting to meet Katherine. I also knew that Madeline and Marissa would be so excited and I didn't want to spoil the excitement. This homecoming would be different in so many ways. Terry wasn't with me. I was exhausted and I had a very sick baby with me. It was post 9/11 and due to new security measures, people greeting us had to wait in the main lobby of the airport. I just wanted to slip out through a back door at the gate.

Due to people's relaxed summer schedules, the early evening hour and the good weather, there were dozens of people at the airport to greet us. Our parents, siblings, aunts and uncles, nieces and nephews, friends and of course, Terry, Marissa and Madeline. I was holding Katherine and a carry-on bag. I heard the loud shouts and cheers before I came around the corner into the main airport lobby. Katherine was so frightened and startled. We didn't know this about her yet, but she hates having a crowd of people direct their attention to her. She hid her face on my shoulder and wouldn't look at anyone.

Terry and the girls approached us first and he pried her from my arms so I could embrace Marissa and Madeline. They were so excited to see me and the baby. I took Katherine back into my arms and we had everyone greet her. She couldn't smile or laugh or anything. She was shot.

She did love looking at all the balloons and after several minutes, warmed up enough for us to pass her around to a few people so they could meet her. Finally, she offered up a smile for our nephew, Sean, and his face revealed a sense of pride and happiness that she had a connection with him.

I felt bad for everyone who came out to the airport because the welcoming party was cut short so we could get Katherine home.

Terry, the three girls and I got into our new van. I had never ridden in it before that night. We purchased it and immediately left to go on our second trip. Joanne used it with Marissa and Madeline while we were away. Anyway, I sat in the back, between Marissa and Madeline's car seats. We were all holding hands.

Marissa was so relieved to have us all back together. She was stroking my hand and she said "Mom, when you're older, you'll never have to go into a nursing home. I'm going to take care of you." Our elderly neighbor had recently moved into an assisted living facility and just before our trip, I took the girls to visit her. At five years old, Marissa was already thinking about her adulthood and drawing parallels with our neighbor's old age living situation.

Just then Madeline turned to me and asked "Mom, can we go to the Drive-In movies tonight?"

That summed up their personalities!

We got home and after we put Katherine to bed, I tried to rest. It was a warm summer night and as usual, all of our bedroom windows were open. Katherine woke up a few hours later and had the first of many night terrors. She wasn't just crying. She was screaming in terror. Her screams rang out through the still neighborhood. We couldn't calm her down, we held her, walked with her, tried rocking her but she wasn't awake and she was screaming.

When she finally calmed down at three o'clock in the morning, Terry, Marissa and I took her downstairs and Marissa fed her a bottle, after which she fell back asleep for a few hours. At seven-thirty in the morning, I called our pediatrician who told me to bring her in immediately, and he'd meet me at the office.

Katherine was diagnosed with a double ear infection and the doctor put her on an antibiotic. Back at the cottage, I was so exhausted that as I was standing in the kitchen, the floor beneath my feet seemed to be moving when I looked down. I realized I had been awake for almost two days. Joanne and Terry took over the baby and kids duty while I fell into a deep slumber upstairs.

Katherine felt better within a day or so, but the terrors continued for several weeks. Sometimes they were caused by her dreams and sometimes by Madeline, eager to be with her new sister, who would crawl into her crib and startle her awake. Katherine was never formally diagnosed but we wondered if she was suffering from a form of PTSD. She was happy and content, but anything or anyone new caused her to shrink into our chest or shoulders.

One day, Terry's sister Kathy asked our next door neighbor if he met the new baby yet. He answered, "Oh yes, we hear her every night!" We felt bad, but without air conditioning at the cottage, there was nothing we could do.

Terry finished up his case and I'm happy to report that he won. He got a favorable result for his client, so leaving early from Russia was worth it.

We settled into life as a family of five and had a great summer.

Again, we received dozens and dozens of cards, gifts, notes and mementos. I got busy writing thank you notes and began planning her upcoming birthday and baptism, both of which were only a few weeks away, in August.

Two weeks after we got home, we celebrated Katherine's first birthday. A big crowd of family gathered around her and sang "Happy Birthday" to her. This was the wrong thing to do. She looked at me and burst into tears. She begged to be held, so I did and she hid her face in my shoulder. She couldn't calm down. She heaved and hiccupped even after her crying subsided. You would think we'd have learned from the airport homecoming that she hated a big crowd looking at her, but we hadn't. Anyway, that was the last time we ever attempted to sing to her on her birthday. Some years, she allowed us to whisper the song, but most years we've only been able to say "Happy Birthday" and then she blows her candles out. To this day, we don't sing to her and she's never allowed us to host a birthday party for her.

We had Katherine baptized on a sunny and warm summer day in late August. We went to St. Anthony's, a little country church out by the cottage. We had a beautiful catered luncheon for about fifty of our family members under a tent in the cottage backyard. The white tent was decorated with pink tulle and flowers and I rented white tablecloths and chairs. It was such a lovely and special day.

Katherine, like her two big sisters, wore the baptismal gown my mother had sewn for the girls five years earlier. Getting ready for church, I left three-year-old Madeline alone on the front porch with Katherine for two minutes with strict instructions not to pick her up. I came back into the room and poor Katherine had a big, red brush burn on the center of her forehead while Madeline tried to convince me that, "Really, Mom, I didn't pick up the baby!"

Chapter TWENTY ONE

Marissa started kindergarten that fall and Madeline started preschool. We closed up the cottage, moved back to Orchard Park and fell into the school routine that we'd happily follow for the next thirteen years, until the college years started.

We adopted Katherine in Erie County Surrogate's Court in September and began our monthly post placement reports for EAC. We watched Katherine get stronger as the weeks passed by and we watched the bonds form between all three girls. Their faces brightened up each time they came home from school and Katherine smiled at them.

We began the job of completing the monthly post-placement reports for Katherine, while still being obligated to have a social worker visit once a year for Madeline, who was only three years old, as well. I could intuitively tell that these visits with the social worker were beginning to take a toll on Marissa. Now five years old, she had a sense that this woman, a pleasant and gentle person, was observing and evaluating our family. Marissa would eagerly explain to the woman how happy we all were and that the kids had nice toys and playthings. Marissa was always very observant and saw things other kids her age didn't. She figured out that this woman held the destiny of our family in her pen. She knew, by the woman's constant note taking and the questions she was asking the girls, that she was reporting back to the agency about the welfare of the children. After she'd leave, I would have to reassure Marissa and try to explain that no one was sending them back to Russia, that no one was breaking up our family. I was so relieved when we finished the post placement reports and visit requirements when Katherine turned three years old.

On December 22, Katherine and I dropped Madeline off at preschool. I was talking to the executive director, Mary, telling her I didn't feel that well and hoped it was nothing serious because I was hosting thirty family members for Christmas Eve dinner in a few days. I was suffering from what I thought was an "intestinal bug" but it wasn't that bad. I had no fever or body aches, just occasional intestinal symptoms. I felt this way for about a week but went ahead with Christmas as planned and felt better by New Years Eve.

On January 3, Terry and I went out with my sister Joanne and brother in law, Pete. I felt fine all evening. The next morning, I woke up with the symptoms again, only this time it was worse. The tempo went like that, off and on for several weeks, all the while I was getting worse each time. I had two trips to the doctor, one emergency room visit and finally I was diagnosed with an intestinal parasite. The Erie County Health Department called me with all sorts of questions about restaurants I ate in and the fresh produce I ate, particularly bagged lettuce. He asked if anyone else in the house was ill. I told him that no, they were all fine, and for some reason, I mentioned the kids were all adopted from Russian orphanages.

"Bingo!" he yelled. He explained that the majority of kids from the Russian orphanages had parasites as part of their normal flora and that is why they weren't symptomatic. I had caught it from Katherine. I looked back at the form from Dr. Chasnoff at the Child Study Center in Chicago. It listed all the recommended tests for the newly adopted babies, once they were home. Down toward the bottom of the list? Ova and parasites. For some reason, we never had that test done.

I was so sick that I lost fourteen pounds. We tested all the girls and had to treat two of the three who tested positive. For me, the first round of a strong antibiotic did nothing. I was getting nervous. The second round finally kicked it, but that wasn't until March rolled around. It was a frightening, annoying and long ordeal.

That spring, Terry and I were casually considering adopting a fourth baby the following year. By now we were forty years old. The Russian government required three trips per each adoption by then. However difficult that sounded, the memory of all those orphans in need of parents was very compelling. It was nearly impossible to let those feelings go. I confided in a close friend. I'll never forget how she answered.

She said, "Oh my god. The last experience nearly killed you. What are you thinking?"

She was absolutely right. Our Russian adoption days were over.

Five years with five trips and ten flights, a boatload of adventures, mountains of paperwork, anxiety and uncertainty, abundant tears, joy and love all culminated in the creation of our beautiful family of five. It would stay that way and it was the perfect size for us.

EPILOGUE

ONE

When Madeline and Katherine were twelve and ten years old, respectively, they needed new passports since theirs had expired. When applying for them, I realized with panic that I never completed their N-600 forms when we adopted them. The N-600 form is the application for a Certificate of Citizenship. There are a few reasons why this slipped past me. First, Marissa participated in the citizenship ceremony at the Buffalo Zoo and we completed her paperwork in preparation for that. Second, the local Immigration office discontinued the citizenship ceremonies, so there never were reminders to fill out the forms. Madeline and Katherine never "ceremoniously" became U.S. citizens. Third, by the time we adopted Madeline, the law had changed to make adopted kids citizens automatically when they landed in the United States leading me to mistakenly believe there was no more paperwork to be completed.

Consequently, in 2012, both Madeline and Katherine were still here on Green Cards, which are permanent resident cards for immigrants. They were U.S. citizens, not permanent residents. I dug out the old paperwork, filed the N-600s, paid the fees and had to provide extensive supporting documentation such as their baptismal certificates, report cards, our marriage license, the deed to our house, etc. I couldn't believe I was back at the paperwork game, after leaving it behind for nine years. They got their certificates, but the pictures on them are not cute little baby pictures; rather they show them in their Nativity School uniforms, slightly messy after a long, active day at school.

TWO

Every year, when we celebrated the girls' birthdays, I thought of their birth mothers. At night, on their birthdays, we'd remember to say a prayer, thanking their birth mothers for giving them their lives.

We also celebrated their Adoption Days each year. We called this their "Gotcha Day," meaning it was the day we "got them." I prepared their favorite meal, we gave them a special but modest gift and then we looked at pictures of their adoptions and reminisced about the experience. We all came to love Gotcha Days, because they were very special, private affairs. EAC, our agency, gave us the idea to celebrate Gotcha Days to help remove any stigma the children may have felt about being adopted. Interestingly, we experienced just the opposite. They seemed to carry their Russian heritage and their adoptions as badges of honor.

One day, in second grade, Marissa told some boys in her class that she was a good hockey player because she was Russian. Later, when I came to school to get her, the boys rushed up to me and asked if she was REALLY Russian. When I replied "yes," they were in awe and said things like "wow" and "cool!" It was so cute.

Despite our celebrating their adoptions, our openness about the process and our willingness to talk freely with them, each of the girls, at times, has carried a small element of sadness or longing with them. I discovered this by little things they'd say, or had written in a short story. A few times, I realized they had rifled through the adoption paperwork without me. I also found little notes they wrote and placed in their nightstands. This was never anything too worrisome or anything that caused undue sadness or pain. It just simply was something that existed. That's all.

When the girls were young and in elementary school, we were at dinner one evening when Terry asked the girls a question. "Girls, what would you do if Jesus was here at our dinner table, right now?"

"That's easy!" yelled Madeline. "I'd show him my stuffed animal collection."

Marissa retorted, "You're an idiot Madeline. I'd ask him if I had any birth siblings and if they were any good at sports, like me."

Terry and I were taken by surprise and we talked later about how that must have been weighing on her mind because she was so specific about her question.

The next night, Terry tried to draw more information out of her while tucking her into bed.

He asked her "Marissa, if you had one wish, what would it be?" Her answer was that the Buffalo Bills would win the Super Bowl.

"No, no," he said, "another wish."

Her answer? That the Buffalo Sabres would win the Stanley Cup.

"No, no, another wish." He said, getting a little exasperated.

She thought quietly for a few minutes and then said, "That New York State would lower the driving age to ten."

So much for her dwelling on what we thought was a big deal. We laughed about that exchange for many years.

Here's an interesting side note: Throughout the years, our girls have met kids at school or in social situations who were adopted from the same regions they are from. This was because many of us used Baker Victory Services as our social worker agency and Baker Victory contracted the placement to EAC in Cleveland. EAC only was certified in a few regions so many kids locally are from the same area in Russia.

THREE

Adoption is a life altering experience. Without loss, there would be no adoption. There is a loss of the birth family, their culture, language, anyone with a physical resemblance and there is the loss of medical information.

The loss they experienced wasn't a one-time event. Their adoptions were something they'd have to reveal any time they went to a new doctor or specialist and family history was required on a form. It came up periodically in school when doing a science lesson in heredity or a religion lesson about a family tree. Sometimes, it would come up at random times while talking to people about where they inherited certain traits like height or a certain skill.

A benefit of them being Russian is that they look like Terry and me, which enables them to share their origin stories, if and when they choose. Their outward appearance doesn't tell their origin story for them and this has preserved some agency for them.

Madeline is frequently told she looks like me and she just laughs and says "yes." She rarely chooses to tell people we aren't biologically related. How much is nature vs. nurture? Whole books have been written on that subject.

Growing up, they'd hear all kinds of comments from people that sometimes gave them pause. They would be asked if they knew how to speak Russian or if they knew who their "real" mothers were. Later, I'd pinch my arm and laughingly say to them, "I'm real. I'm not fake or a cartoon!" Interestingly, they were never asked about their "real" fathers. We all understood people meant no harm and the girls learned to navigate such situations and take them in stride. Katherine once laughingly said, "People just don't get it!" When they were younger, I frequently had other women say to me, in front of the girls, "Your girls are so cute! I'd do that! I'd adopt a baby from Russia!" This struck me as odd, as if they were a particularly cute sweater I picked up at a boutique.

Their adoptions also brought me an awareness of how often people say things like "blood is thicker than water" and " they're blood relatives." To this I say, we are living testimony that LOVE is thicker than BLOOD. And what's the big deal about blood anyway? It stains things sometimes, literally and figuratively.

The girls gave me a Christmas gift one year that was a frame with a handwritten saying about family and how God chooses your family for you. I keep it by my bathroom sink and read it every day.

As they've aged, we've had discussions about family, children and faith. One of them recently questioned her belief in God. I responded that I firmly believe it was God who brought us together from across the world to be a family and that is one reason I believe in God. I reminded her that belief in God has nothing to do with agreeing with the laws of man made religions. She thought about it and came back to me later, agreeing with my thinking at that time. What her beliefs are now, I am uncertain.

It's not all a "happy" adoption story. Yes, we consistently choose to think of it in terms of happiness, but sometimes, while they were experiencing some particular troubles, I felt that love wasn't enough to fill the void they felt. I read an article about adoption that said people talk about adopted kids being "chosen." Well, some could argue that you have to be "unchosen" first in order to be chosen. This concept can create an emptiness in some adopted children. They require not only love, but validation and support as well.

Because of this, I decided to make raising them my life's work. Terry was committed to working long hours at his law firm and what little free time he did have, he spent it on things like reading them books, teaching them to swim or ride bikes, shooting countless hockey pucks and basketball hoops with them in the driveway or fishing down at our neighborhood pond. Because of him, all three girls have surprised their guy friends by knowing how to throw a perfect spiral football.

I made a commitment to stay at home and not work full-time. I know this is an unpopular choice by today's standards. I realized we were fortunate to have the financial stability for me to make this choice. However, at different times throughout the years, I have felt a deep sense of longing for my career and struggled to find community. I've seen my friends and colleagues go on to corporate leadership positions. I was conflicted because I was told, by our culture, that a woman "can have it all." I didn't feel like I wanted it all. I wanted to be "all in" with raising them. I was always careful not to lose myself or have myself disappear into their identities. When talking to people, sometimes I feel an inadequacy that I've chosen what looks like the much-maligned 1950s housewife role. I understand this feeling of inadequacy may be my ego talking.

Even though I've worked "part time, no time and sometimes" throughout the last twenty years and despite staying active in community work, I still find myself explaining or rationalizing my choice to others. This is silly, but I do it.

We felt that the girls needed a positive, constant role model to provide them a sense of belonging. By being there, day after day, with the house warm and the lights on when they got off the bus, I was trying to replace their "longing" with "belonging." We believe that parental commitment plays an important role in holding adoptions together.

Some people have asked me why I didn't go back to work once they were older. I did indeed plan to do that, however, it was precisely when they were older that they needed me most. When they became teenagers, they experienced an awakening and saw their situation in a different light. Yes, they had happy and carefree childhoods, but they thought about their beginnings in ways they hadn't before.

As an example, Madeline was a sophomore in high school when she realized she was then the age her biological mother had been when she gave birth to her. It wasn't until they matured that they began to fully appreciate their origins and the loss that came with that. If asked, they'll tell you they rarely felt this way, but I wanted to be there, in case they did. We always celebrated the joy and happiness associated with their adoptions and never focused on the negative aspects. Up until they were teenagers, they were too young to understand what happened to them.

People frequently ask me if the girls want to go back to Russia. In fact, someone in my writing class asked me this very question. My answer is always the same, long answer. First, the United States government only recognizes single citizenship and they are U.S. citizens. However, the Russian government considers them to have retained their Russian citizenship as well. If we went to Russia, they would be required to enter Russia on their Russian passports. This makes us uneasy and we've communicated such to the girls. Second, we would take the girls back to Russia, if they wanted to go. However, I would want to know WHY they wanted to go to Russia. If they wanted to experience their culture or see the country, we would support them and take them to Russia. On the other hand, we would not rush to take them if they were interested in chasing a fantasy of finding their long-lost birth families. Many people have chosen to find their adopted children's birth families. We aren't those people. Terry and I don't believe that curiosity is a good enough reason to disrupt strangers' lives.

Their birth mothers gave us all an incredible gift. Can't we just leave well enough alone? We also thought tracking down birth families would invite unnecessary stress and drama into the girls' developing lives and identities. They certainly didn't need that. So far, none of them have expressed a great desire to go to Russia. We will support them in whatever decision they come to make as adults about Russia and birth families. Our feelings are our own and they are just now becoming adults and can form their own opinions.

We are profoundly grateful that their birth mothers gave them life and in turn, allowed us to teach them how to live that life. I had a little poem on the dresser in the nursery that read: "Not flesh of my flesh, nor bone of my bone, but still miraculously my own. Never forget for a minute, you didn't grow under my heart, but in it."

FOUR

Back when I spoke at Russian adoption seminars, I would tell prospective parents that adopting children from Russia was not for the faint of heart. The process was long, expensive, stressful and complicated. This can also be said for raising the children, once the adoption is finalized. Our girls all came with what Terry and I referred to as "The Orphanage Hangover." These were subtle manifestations in their behavior that pointed to clues about the lasting effect of their time spent in orphanages. There are so many times Terry and I shared this thought. We would identify a pattern of behavior or a trait of their personality and wonder if that was a result of their time in an institution.

I've read several articles and studies about the long term effects of being neglected as an infant. The bond a baby makes with her mother is essential and not having that can result in long term effects such as low self-esteem, anxiety and attention disorders, to name a few. We saw the immediate effects of chronic neglect in each of the girls: a flat head due to hours lying in a crib, self-stimulation such as finger play, not crying or fussing upon waking up, failure to thrive, and delays in motor skills.

I will provide a story here to illustrate:

As a toddler, Katherine was completely unable to look adults in the eye. She would hide her face in our shoulders when meeting new people. She would make herself small, folding her arms and hunching her shoulders, when confronted with anything new. She disdained having a group of people looking at her. Was this behavior a result of her being eleven-and-a-half months old when we adopted her? Was it a result of losing her birth mother at six months old? Was it from living in an institution for six months? Was this post-traumatic stress? We'll never know for certain why Katherine was like that. We just dealt with the problem and discovered that putting her on a horse at four years old solved most of the issues. She needed to speak up and be in charge of that horse and the lessons she learned spilled over into other areas of her life. Learning to bravely advocate for herself has been an ongoing process and started with her horseback riding. She is still riding today, at seventeen years old, and is very poised and self-assured when speaking to adults.

Throughout the years, we never used their humble beginnings as a crutch or an excuse for poor behavior. We chose to keep our eyes looking forward to the future. This enabled us to have what I call the "It's all gravy!" mindset. Each one of the girls achieved an incredible accomplishment: they survived their ordeals in their orphanages, they came here and they thrived. It's all gravy after that! Terry and I have frequently reminded them of their resolve and resiliency. They know that no matter what life throws their way, they can and will persevere. They are strong and I've worked hard to make sure they know that.

FIVE

In December 2012, Russian President Vladimir Putin banned all Americans from adopting children from Russia. To fully comprehend why this happened, I recommend reading Bill Browder's book, *Red Notice*. It's a comprehensive and compelling account of alleged corruption in Russia.

From 1991 to 2012, over fifty thousand Russian orphans were adopted by American families. Seventy percent of these children arrived in the 1990s. Gradually, the process started to get more difficult and the numbers began dropping off. By the time the ban went into effect, one thousand children were in the process of being adopted by Americans. Tragically, their adoptions never moved forward and they were left stranded in the Russian orphanage system, their broken-hearted American families left with a forever hole in their souls.

Some believe that Putin put the ban in place as retaliation for a U.S. law that imposed sanctions on Russian officials who were accused of human rights violations. The law is called the Magnitsky Act, so named after Bill Browder's tax advisor Sergei Magnitsky.

Magnitsky alleged there was widespread corruption in Russia. He was arrested and subsequently died while in police custody. U.S. President Barack Obama enacted the Magnitsky Act, which barred those Russian officials believed to be involved with corruption and human rights violations from entering the U.S. and from using the U.S. banking system, freezing their assets held in U.S. banks. In response, Russia retaliated by banning all adoptions by American families.

During the 2016 U.S. Presidential election, there was widespread media coverage of Donald Trump, Jr. and other Trump campaign officials meeting with a Russian lawyer named Natalia Veselnitskaya in Trump Tower in New York. Donald Trump, Jr. went on record, claiming they only discussed Russian adoptions.[12] I don't know what the truth is, but I believe that there is no way they'd be discussing adoptions without talking about the possibility of repealing the Magnitsky Act. That didn't happen and in fact, it's been expanded and is now called The Global Magnitsky Act.

So what happened to the Russian children living in orphanages? We don't know. The Russian Government has stated that there are some foster care homes in Russia now and that some of the children have been adopted by Russian families. Human Rights Watch isn't convinced of the truth of these statements. In 2012, at the time of the ban, there were over two thousand one hundred orphanages in Russia. Russia has not released any information about how many exist today. Allegedly, there is a public education program in place to dispel Russian's deep-rooted prejudices against abandoned children.

I have no way of checking on the orphans or the orphanage system itself. Our agency, European Adoption Consultants (EAC) was raided by the FBI in 2017 and shut down and barred by the U.S. State Department from conducting international adoptions. An employee of the agency pled guilty to offering bribes to Ugandan officials and coordinating illegal adoptions from Uganda.

While the adoptions worked out very well for the five of us, that was not the case for some people. One couple we knew went to get a second baby a few years after their first baby. They arrived in Russia to discover that their new baby had died. They were heartbroken and started the process all over again, which culminated in the adoption of a baby boy. Another couple we know decided not to use the agency for their second baby and used a less expensive private attorney instead. They ended up coming home with a child older than their first child. Another family found the institutional behaviors of their daughter too dangerous and destructive and sadly, had to institutionalize her for her safety as well as their own. Another family couldn't handle their child's behaviors caused by the severe emotional deprivation and neglect and ended up "re-adopting" the child, meaning, they gave the child up for adoption to another family here in the U.S. Three of the couples we interacted with during the process had their marriages end in divorce. These are just cases we know of, personally. There were a few widely publicized cases nationally. One mother, so overwhelmed by the issues and behaviors, tragically sent her child back to Russia on a plane alone. Putin used this case to publicly justify the ban in 2012.

SIX

I can't use enough superlatives and hyperbole to describe what a dream come true it's been for us. Adoption is a wonderful way to build a family but indeed, it's not easy. It's taken work, patience, commitment and a lot of love. The adventures we have had along the way have been great fodder for conversation and have turned into family legends. In the end, we've been so abundantly blessed with our family of five. The three girls have unique origin stories, making them the strong, beautiful, young women they are today. They represent the best that any parent could ever ask for in daughters. Of course, we've had problems and issues, just like all families. Some days were long and there were periods of time I was filled with angst and despair. I even came down with shingles once in response to a particularly difficult time in one of the girl's lives. But like most families, overall, we've had a wonderful, love-filled life. All the stories about the trips to Russia, the worries we had about the process, the anxiety we felt during the adoptions were all worth it and we'd build our family this way again, in a heartbeat. It's been an honor to be their mother and a privilege to raise them.

IMAGES

Jeannine & Terry, Senior Prom, 1982

Jeannine & Terry at their wedding

Little Tykes Cozy Coupe

Hotel Ukraina

Jeannine & Terry, Moscow, 1998 (First trip to Russia, Meeting Marissa)

Backyard of Murom Infant Home

Terry holding Marissa for the first time

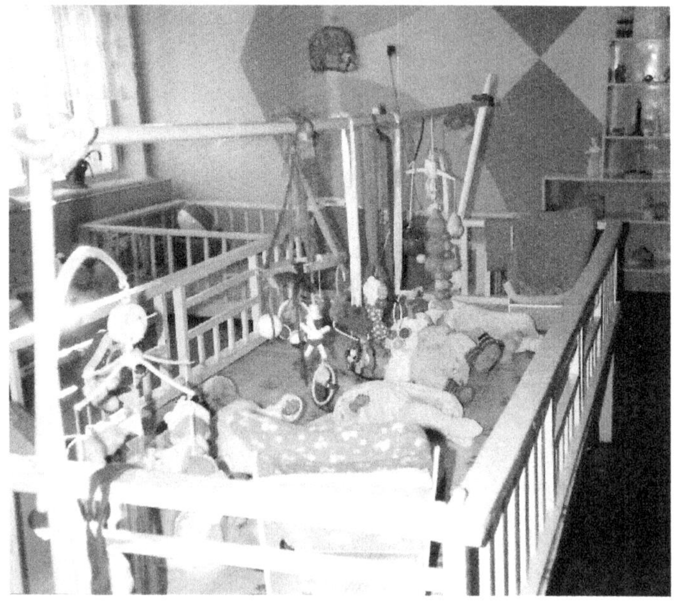

Babies in the Murom Infant Home

Marissa's homecoming

Marissa on her second day home

Terry in the train compartment, 2001 (Meeting Madeline)

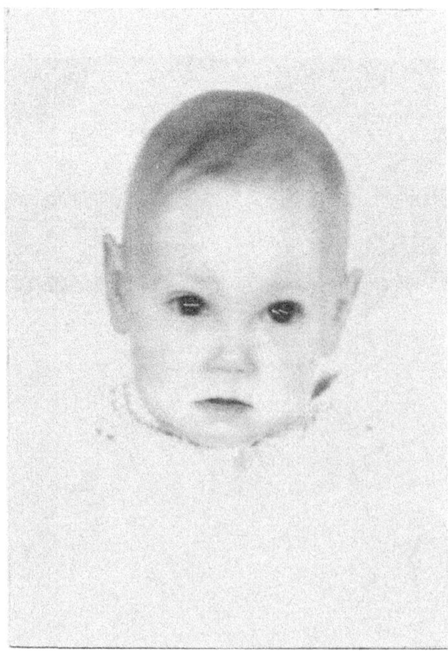

Madeline's picture from the computer screen at the Ministry of Education

Krasny Bor Baby House

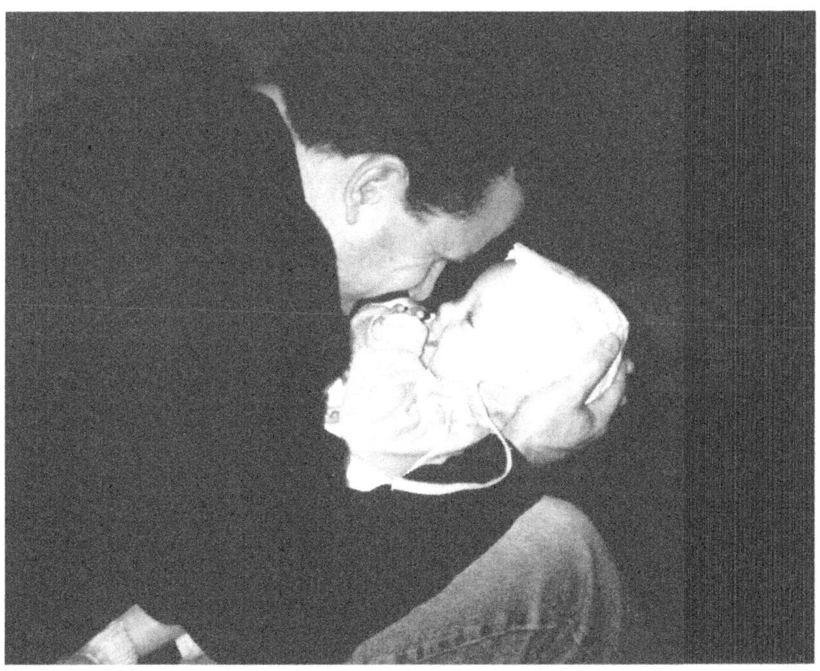

Terry & Maddy, getting to know each other and sharing a remarkable laugh

Terry holding Maddy before heading back to Moscow

Madeline's homecoming, Buffalo Airport, 2001

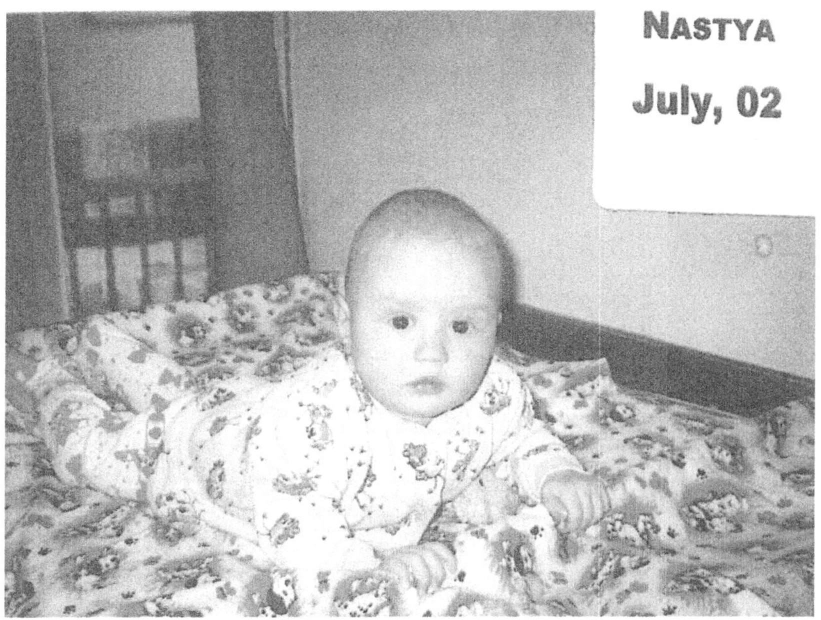

Katherine's referral photo

Jeannine meeting Katherine, 2003

Jeannine & Terry at the Hotel in Vladimir, 2003

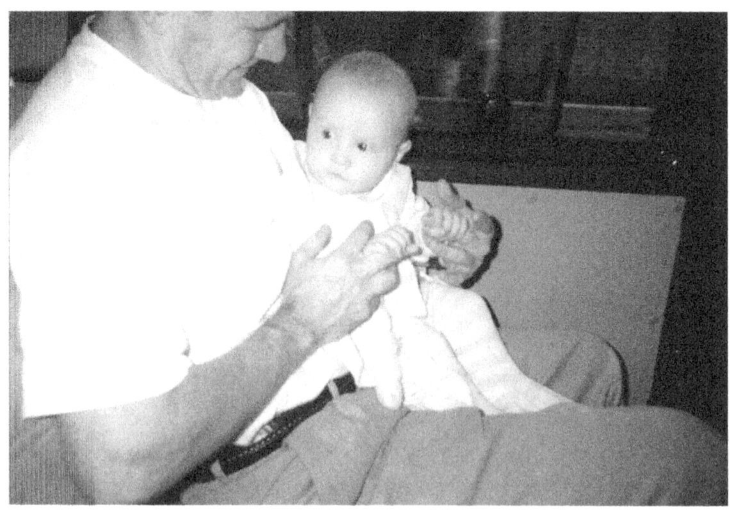

Katherine in the van, leaving orphanage (no seat belts or car seats), 2003

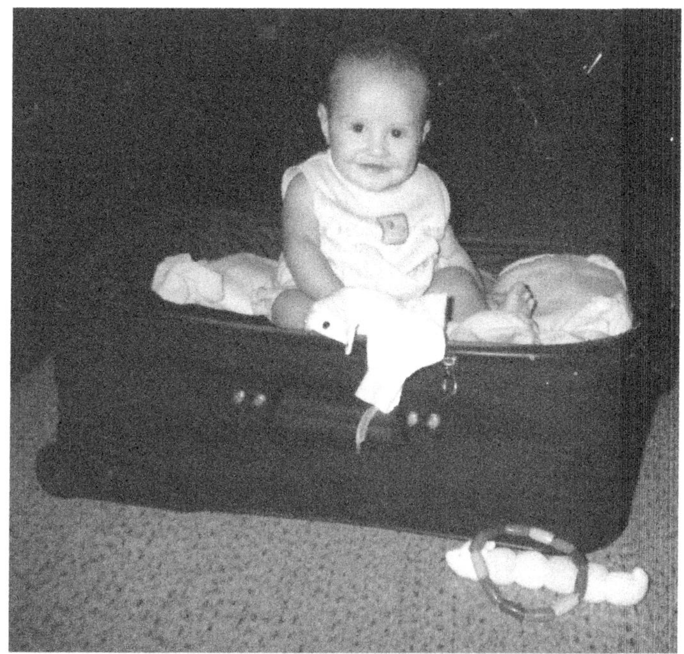

Katherine, playing in her suitcase before going home, 2003

Katherine's homecoming, Buffalo Airport, 2003

Katherine's Baptism day, 2003

Jeannine, Marissa, Katherine, andMadeline

From left to right: Katherine Claire, Madeline Grace, and Marissa Jeannine
July 2019

ACKNOWLEDGEMENTS

On New Year's Eve, December 2019, while in Florida, I told Terry, Marissa and Katherine that I was going to write a book about the girl's adoptions. They were all immediately supportive, but surprised. Were they skeptical that I'd actually do it? I'm not sure. I was committed to the idea but wasn't sure at that point how I was going to accomplish writing a book. I was fortunate that I journaled while on each trip and those little notebooks served as the basis for this book.

The first person I'd like to acknowledge is Terry. His interest sustained me throughout the process. The girls, Marissa Jeannine, Madeline Grace and Katherine Claire, for always offering me encouragement. They appeared to be intrigued when I told them I spent the day writing about them. I also discovered that they talked with pride about my writing to others. To my friend, Coleen Scott who, back in January when I asked her how I should get started, told me to enroll in my writing class. That was the catalyst to get me going. My first class was Tuesday morning, February 7, 2020. We met weekly for four months. I'd like to thank Rick Ohler, the instructor for his interest, guidance, encouragement and his editing skills. I'd like to acknowledge the women in my writing class. They were such enthusiastic listeners during our weekly in-person and then our COVID-19 ZOOM classes. I always appreciated their patience and discretion when I got emotional, reading some passages out loud for the first time. They provided such a safe and supportive environment and they each have wonderful, rich stories of their own. A special shout out to my friend, Kelly Griffin, who agreed to be my "TR" or Trusted Reader before the book went to the editing phase. Finally and most importantly, a very special acknowledgement to the girls' birthmothers. They not only gave the girls their lives but they made it possible for us to create a wonderful family, the Higgins Family, and for that I'm eternally grateful.

Thank you all.

Jeannine Higgins

May 28, 2020

FOOTNOTES

[1] Jennifer S. Jones, "How Does Life in an Orphanage Affect a Child's Development?" Adoption.org

[2] Associated Press. " Younger Workers in Russia Found More Likely to Be Poor." The New York Times, November 19, 1998, Section A, Page 5

[3] Mark G. Field. Russia's Torn Safety Nets: Health and Social Welfare During the Transition, (U.S., Palgrave Macmillan, 2000)

[4]Tomasz Wites. "Abortions in Russia Before and After the Fall of the Soviet Union." University of Warsaw, 2004

[5] Fred Hiatt. "Russia's Unwanted Children Being Adopted by West." Washington Post, February 18, 1992. https://www.washingtonpost.com

[6]The Henry M. Jackson School of International Studies. University of Washington. Russia in the 1990s: Independence and the Yeltsin Years. jsis.washington.edu

[7] Human Rights Watch. Cruelty and Neglect in Russian Orphanages. 1998. www.hrw.org

[8] Eurasia Foundation. In Foster Care Reform, American and Russian Experts Converge. April 8, 2015. www.eurasia.org

[9] "Russian Adoption: A Brief History & What's Behind the Media Attention." Adoptive Families Magazine (July 14, 2017)

[10] Swift, John. "Battle of Smolensk. Napoleonic Wars 1812." Brittanica

[11] Their names have been changed to protect their privacy.

[12] All Things Considered, Russian Ban on US Adoptions Become Embroiled in Trump Controversy, NPR, July 20, 2017

Made in the USA
Middletown, DE
20 December 2022

19886771R00086